Stonehenge

A New Look at the Oldest Mystery in the World

(Solving the Mysteries of the Greatest Stone Age Monument)

Cynthia Medina

Published By **Tyson Maxwell**

Cynthia Medina

All Rights Reserved

Stonehenge: A New Look at the Oldest Mystery in the World (Solving the Mysteries of the Greatest Stone Age Monument)

ISBN 978-1-77485-534-8

No part of this guidebook shall be reproduced in any form without permission in writing from the publisher except in the case of brief quotations embodied in critical articles or reviews.

Legal & Disclaimer

The information contained in this ebook is not designed to replace or take the place of any form of medicine or professional medical advice. The information in this ebook has been provided for educational & entertainment purposes only.

The information contained in this book has been compiled from sources deemed reliable, and it is accurate to the best of the Author's knowledge; however, the Author cannot guarantee its accuracy and validity and cannot be held liable for any errors or omissions. Changes are periodically made to this book. You must consult your doctor or get professional medical advice before using any of the suggested remedies, techniques, or information in this book.

Upon using the information contained in this book, you agree to hold harmless the Author from and against any damages, costs, and expenses, including any legal fees potentially resulting from the application of any of the information provided by this guide. This disclaimer applies to any damages or injury caused by the use and application, whether directly or indirectly, of any advice or information presented, whether for breach of contract, tort, negligence, personal injury, criminal intent, or under any other cause of action.

You agree to accept all risks of using the information presented inside this book. You need to consult a professional medical practitioner in order to ensure you are both able and healthy enough to participate in this program.

Table Of Contents

Introduction _____ 1

Chapter 1: Physical Description _____ 4

Chapter 2: Archaeological Work _____ 18

Chapter 3: Folklore And History _____ 33

Chapter 4: The Tourism And Context ___ 53

Chapter 5: Intrigue And Mystery _____ 61

Chapter 6: Importance Of Stonehenge _ 71

Chapter 7: Stonehenge's Purpose _____ 86

Chapter 8: Study As Well As Excavations Of Stonehenge_____ 100

Chapter 9: Stonehenge's Position Within The Landscape _____ 112

Chapter 10: Stonehenge Folklore _____ 125

Chapter 11: Short Overview Of The Major Phases Of Stonehenge _____ 136

Conclusion _____ 164

Introduction

Over the years, historians who are professionals have fought the arduous job of capturing the history of our time as accurately as they can but even with the most modern technology, archaeology and archives, some questions have been unable to find the answers. From the beginnings to the origins of Atlantis and The Lost Colony in Roanoke The mysteries surrounding some of the most famous individuals and events have intrigued many generations.

The Salisbury Plain, only a few hours away from the bustle and hustle that is Central London, remains one of the most important remaining relics from the world's past time: the massive stones of Stonehenge. Stonehenge is among the most popular old-fashioned sites in the world and the image of it can trigger a myriad of emotional and psychological responses. Its beauty stems not only due to its size and impressive degree in preservation but even more than that, it is due to the astonishing accuracy with which Stonehenge was constructed in an age of technology that was simple and social structure. It is evidently an important place to be in - then and today.

Despite its serene, unchanging style, Stonehenge has been a site of ideological, political and religious conflict over the decades. From the heated debates of the 19th century's theorists to the all-night dancing celebrations of the 1980s the past and present of Stonehenge is as much about the needs and anxieties of the citizens of contemporary Britain and the past. Stonehenge is a part of everyone in Britain since the time it was built around 5500 years ago. it has been a part of the unfolding story.

Of of course, Stonehenge has long fascinated all over the world and continues to seek to comprehend every aspect of the place and the reason behind the site. This requires a thorough understanding of the reasons Stonehenge is situated in the first place and what the stones are made of and what archaeology research has revealed concerning the people that constructed Stonehenge. In addition, Stonehenge is a center of folklore and mythology that has changed in time, and has become the basis for a distinct religious system of belief that acknowledges Stonehenge as the "living Temple" and contests the official guardianship of the area.

The Greatest of History's Mysteries: Stonehenge comprehensively covers the details, mysteries, and theories that surround the megalithic site of ancient times. Readers will comprehend Stonehenge from all angles as a physical site as well as an object of academic study, a location of worship and ecstatic celebration as well as an unmissable "must be seen" top tourist attraction and an iconic symbol of both culture and history. Alongside images and a bibliography the reader will be able to learn about Stonehenge unlike you've ever before, and in the shortest amount of time.

Chapter 1: Physical Description

An outline of Stonehenge and its diverse physical features, drawn by Anthony Johnson

"Salisbury Cathedral as well as its neighbor Stonehenge are two famous monuments to the arts and indignity They may also be the first essay as well as the final perfect architectural design." A letter was written by the Dr. Johnson in 1783.

Although there is much debate about the origins and the future of Stonehenge however, there is a common understanding of the exact nature of Stonehenge an impressive megalithic structure in Britain and perhaps the entire world. Furthermore there is a consensus that the Stonehenge you have today is not the work of a single creator or even a single civilization, but rather an important site for millennia, if not centuries.

Before the construction started at the site that is now known as Stonehenge the people living nearby were working. Archaeology has revealed the existence of constructions that utilized posts made of wood dating to around 8000 B.C. The posts were east-west alignment that was similar to those similar to those that were found in Scandinavia however, they were not found in Britain itself.

Around 5,500 years ago it was believed that about 5,500 years ago, Stonehenge Cursus was built just a little under a half mile north of Stonehenge perhaps because woods were removed by farmers in this direction, as the area growing. The Cursus is a ditch that's an entire mile and around 150 feet wide and its location, which was initially believed to have been an Ancient Roman race track gave it the name cursus (Latin meaning "course"). One of the tools employed to create the path was discovered by archaeologists who could radiocarbonly date it to around fourth millennium B.C.

The Stonehenge Cursus

The first Stonehenge constructed around 5,000 years ago, is believed to be an earthen circle and ditch referred to as"embankment" "embankment". The wall and ditch were more than 350 feet and had two entrances, one in the south and the other in the northeast. Archaeology discovered animal bones and tools, however the fact that bones and tools were not identical in age suggested that the area was used to bury people.

The outside of the structure was dotted with 56 pits in a circle inside the embankment. it is believed to be home to 56 posts made of wood in addition to the pits. They were referred to as Aubrey Holes in honor of John Aubrey, a 17th century man who was a specialist in antiques and who first noticed the existence of pits. Many believe that the pits contained one of the initial "blue stones" meaning that the stone construction began at Stonehenge around 500 years earlier than is commonly accepted nowadays. However, the majority of individuals believe that posts made of wood and the wooden structures built inside the circle were taken away at the time the first stones started being used around 2600 B.C.

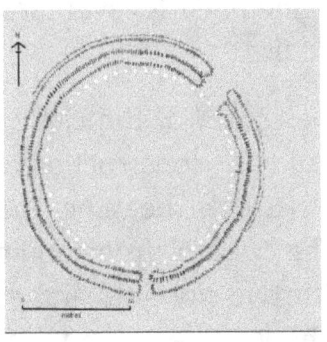

Diagram of the original construction of Stonehenge is often called Stonehenge 1.

Instead of wood structures built by the builders, they created two semi-circles from small "blue stones" but they were replaced just one century later by the full circle of powerful Sarsen stones. The upright stones were about 25 tons in weight and are believed to originated from the area of the stone circle in Avebury which was located about 20 miles from the Marlborough Downs. They were used to create an elongated circle of about 100 feet wide. On top of the upright sarsens , were set "lintel" stones that linked the rings. In spite of the fact the structure was constructed on a slope that was slight, the builders managed to alter the sarsens' heights so that the lintels remained nearly level throughout the whole structure.

Then, in the center of the circle is the most powerful of all constructions that is 5 "trilithons" (Greek meaning "having three stone"). They were freestanding trios of stones, with two uprights and a Lintel. The five trilithons were an approximate horseshoe. The lintels of the sarsen circular were about 16 feet higher than their ground level, the largest trilithon stood about 25 feet tall. The engineering required to build the site is impressive when you consider that approximately one third part of every upright's length is dug in the ground.

Trilithons at Stonehenge

The sarsens that are found both in the inner and outer circles are the most striking element of the design. They weren't quarried, and were discovered half-buried in the landscape, remnants from the previous Ice Age. They are made of sands that have been bound with silica, the stones are exceptionally robust and are frequently employed as roadside curbs or stone steps. The stone's ability to be not just transported out of Marlborough Downs but also transported to Marlborough Downs but also shaped into rectangular shapes with only wood, stone or bone tool is testimony to the creativity and commitment of the construction workers.

Graffiti discovered on one of the stone sarsen

In circles, the circle with the sarsen stones as well as the horseshoe inside of trilithons are smaller rings of stones that aren't local and are referred to as "blue stones." They differ in their origins and aren't so meticulously worked as Sarsens. The source of a lot of them can be traced back to an area in southern Wales about 150 miles away. What brought glaciers or humans to the area is debated, since archaeologists have been successful in proving that either is feasible. 150 miles would require Herculean efforts to transport the stones using either land or by water, however it's evident there were some massive stones were transported for nearly two dozen miles further.

Bluestones from Stonehenge

The location of Stonehenge is vital to its creators and its admirers to this day. The trilithons' horseshoe is directly in front of the opening of the embankment. This will lead to an avenue of access. Together the alignment is known by the "Axis" and on the avenue is another sarsen, which is the famous "Heelstone." The trilithons as well as the Avenue as well as the Heelstone are aligned in such a way that on the Summer Solstice (June 21) it rises direct above the Heelstone and, at the Winter Solstice (December 21) it is set between stone fragments of the now demolished central, highest Trilithons. In the same way an increasing amount research suggests the earliest peoples first came to Stonehenge at the time of when it was the Winter Solstice, based in part on the finding of pig's teeth as well as the study of how old the pigs were at the time they were killed.

The Heelstone

The view of Stonehenge at the Heelstone

Although it is possible that other stones are connected to other events of the celestial calendar and that the whole structure was an approximate calendar for the year, these connections are still discussed by archaeologists. Archaeoastronomy is a field (the research of the connection between ancient civilizations and star constellations) at Stonehenge is a contentious area, with both astronomers as well as archaeologists taking sides initially over Stonehenge Decoded (1963) written by Gerald Hawkins, which claimed Stonehenge could be used to forecast eclipses. The debates started long ago, with Edmund Halley studying the placement of the Heelstone and arguing over whether it was an astronomically aligned stone or perhaps by using magnetic Compass.

Stonehenge is situated on Salisbury Plain, a broad high chalkland situated in southwest Britain which is full of ancient sites. Salisbury Plain includes not only the main site of Stonehenge but as well hills, barrows, palisades, and other monuments. According to UNESCO, "they form landscapes that are unmatched" and are currently protected by the World Heritage Site. [1]

This area is often ignored by the tourists of today who focus on the stones however, it was crucial for the builders as well as archaeologists trying to comprehend the context of the society in the context in which Stonehenge was built. The current owner of the area around it which is The National Trust, is working to restore the old ecosystem known as it is a "calcareous (chalk) grassland." The ecosystem is distinguished by the thin layer of soil that is laid over chalk or limestone bedrock, and surrounded by tough grasses. It is noted by its abundant wildflowers and was formed within the Stonehenge area after it was removed of trees. The land is slated to be used for grazing without causing harm to the system, however being that the area is very little fertility has actually helped the area (and particularly the nearby smaller sites) very well, shielding them from destruction by the plow and modern structures that have destroyed archaeological sites across other regions of Britain.

One aspect of recent studies on landscapes has been the huge number of burials in the surrounding hills, which has been long-time associated with Stonehenge in the process. The earliest people, the ones who might have constructed the first embankments or wooden posts, laid their dead in large communal graves like the West Kennet Long Barrow northwest of Stonehenge. In the Barrow (an artificial hill that had burial chambers built within) bones were buried among people with various types of bones that were buried in various rooms.

Additionally, the builders were able move large sarsens around to form an entryway into the tomb, similar to earlier trilithons. But the builders of later Stonehenge laid their bodies in individual barrows made of round stones on the tops of hills, usually in close proximity to the stone henge. The majority of these burials were those of wealthy people which suggests that the region or had a high concentration of wealth or the wealthy wanted for burials near to the famed monument. According to some archaeologists, this area is considered to be the "Lourdes" of prehistoric Europe which attracted (like the present-day French sanctuary) hundreds of wounded and sick seeking healing, especially the wealthy neolithic. A few of them weren't healed, which accounts for the large percentage of burials in the surrounding region that have these kinds of remains. Perhaps the most intriguing thing is archaeologists have not found evidence of burials within the barrows that are located within the Stonehenge site.

Computer-generated renderings of what Stonehenge could look like if it was finished

Chapter 2: Archaeological Work

This photo from World War I shows work being carried out on Stonehenge using wood set up against the stones.

There's never been a time in British history that the significance about Stonehenge disappeared, and unlike other well-known sites such for instance Lascaux Cave in France, Machu Picchu in Peru or Great Zimbabwe, there is no moment of astonishment or the subsequent change in archaeology. In fact, Stonehenge has existed in the consciousness of the public for the entirety of archaeology as a discipline and is largely due because of its proximity to the top universities like Oxford, Cambridge and London, Stonehenge has been intimately with the development of the discipline at each point in its development.

"Early" archaeology at the site is located among the first attempts to apply scientific methods to the remains of the earlier times. The first person to be able to qualify as an "archaeologist" and was also the first to study at the location is John Aubrey.

Aubrey's most famous work is Monumenta Britannica, an attempt to list the stone structures in southern Britain. The book explained Stonehenge in detail, noting holes where the old posts made of wood were placed (now named "Aubrey Holes" in his tribute to his) and also attempting to link the site with the existing textual evidence. He was able to link Stonehenge with the Druids mentioned by Roman chroniclers and a connection that modern researchers have disproved. However, his work was a significant move in bringing people to consider Stonehenge as a place with historical and scientific value and not just one that is used for romantic stories and folklore. [5]

John Aubrey

After Aubrey The next major archaeologist who worked at this site included William Stukeley, who bridged between archaeology and Neo-druidry. For Stukeley was who was an Anglican Priest There was no doubt that the druids constructed the site. And Stukeley and his colleagues (like Iolo Morganwg in Wales) tried to recreate this long-lost "authentic" British religious tradition that he believed was part of an earlier "universal" faith. 6. Stukeley however, was a key figure in the field of archaeology as well, because it was his first attempt to research the dating of the site based on theories now in disrepute concerning the motion in the direction of the magnetic poles. Even though he used flawed science, Stukeley became the very first to identify the alignment of the celestial spheres at the site and even took the first steps of excavation and opening a grave that which he claimed to be the property of an "warrior princess." The most important work of Stukeley on the site was titled Stonehenge as an ancient temple that was ascribed for The British Druids (1740). [7]

Stukeley

At the turn of the century, excavations started to take place not just in Stonehenge but also within all the landscape around, which contained numerous barrows. Two of the most prominent people are William Cunnington and his patron and friend Sir Richard Colt Hoare. Together, and in separate ways both men have excavated hundreds of burials, and dug up the earth surrounding the stone. Although their methods were primitive, and they had to throw out many things that could be extremely valuable to modern archaeologists (including the ashes of campfires as well as bones from both animals and human beings) However, a large portion of the material they found can be used by researchers in the present. Their research Ancient Wiltshire (1812-21) "set the bar for publication of antiquities"[8in the sense that it relied exclusively on the actual findings of excavations and in its detailed analysis of the results and contexts. The discoveries sparked fascination with the ancient past across Britain and helped push archaeology out of the realm of antiquarian doodles to the realm of science that it would eventually become.

Memorial for Hoare within Salisbury Cathedral

The final of these iconic archaeologists working on the area were William Gowland and William Hawley. Gowland did his best to bring back the site in 1901 and Hawley tried to do the same between 1919 and. They stabilized stone and conducted archaeology at the site. They were agents for the state, as their work was funded with public funds. The site had already been popular with tourists mostly because it was a part of Romantic imagery promoted by archaeologists who had previously worked at the site and the state wanted to protect them (from the falling stone) and maintain the site. The work of this kind was taking place in Britain for a long time particularly following the fall of Lanyon Quoit (another type made of stone) located in Cornwall fell in 1815. Lanyon Quoit was rebuilt around 1824, by British naval engineers. They decided to cutting the stones to improve their strength. Similar to that, Gowland re-set one of the stones with concrete and moved it about half a meter away from its original spot.

Gowland

A picture from 1877 of Stonehenge

A photo of Stonehenge from the same angle in the present illustrates the variations caused by reconstruction.

In in the 20th century, archaeology was beginning to develop as a distinct field with the development of typology and stratigraphy. Stratigraphy is the analysis of soil layers of a particular site to determine the time when features were made in relation to one another as well as to the features and artifacts found from other archeological sites. Typology is the study of archaeological artifacts from various sites to identify the relationships (e.g. "people who came from A developed hand axes in style A and pottery style C"). When combined the scientific methods changed archaeology from an investigation of specific sites to permit the understanding of the connections between various sites. In Britain one of the "father" for these methods is William Flinders Petrie, who was a specialist in Egypt but started in his early career working in Stonehenge around the year 1872 (at the age of 19). The technique was further changed thanks to the work of an Australian known as V. Gordon Childe who worked on the ancient ruins of the Scottish Orkney Islands. Childe wanted to turn archaeology into a study of the history of non-literate communities. [10]

Like always, Stonehenge was important in the transformations that took place as well as William Hawley was something of the transitional character. On one hand, he was able to revisit the excavations made by his predecessors by digging up the ground they disturbed, however, there was also an area he referred to as"the "Stonehenge Layer", which was believed to be dated back to the creation of the Sarsens. He was able to identify that many of the structures (like those of the Aubrey Holes) were prior to this construction, which makes the first historian to understand how the area was built over several stages. Actually, a heavily modified version of his chronology continues to be being used to this day. Unfortunately for Hawley his work, it was ignored in his own day.

The multi-stage design that is Stonehenge was further developed, popularized , and then pushed towards the level of consensus of one of 20th Century's most influential Stonehenge archeologists: Richard Atkinson. Beginning in during the 40s Atkinson was involved in excavations at Stonehenge throughout the 1950s, 60s and 70s. He continued to write about it throughout his entire life. His final book on the topic, Stonehenge and Neighboring Monuments released in 1993, just one year before his demise. The year 1979 was the time that Atkinson created a detailed timeline of the development of the Stonehenge site (building on Hawley's basic discoveries) that ran from 2800 BC up to 400 AD . In addition, Atkinson was influential beyond Stonehenge and documented the methods he employed on this site within his book Field Archaeology, which was widely utilized in British archaeological schools and was revised on the 1st of January, 1981 Hyperion Press.

Another field that has produced photographic results, however with little in the form of concrete data is the field of experimental archaeology. It is a subfield of archaeology that tries to recreate the methods and tools used by the ancient civilizations. It first gained traction in 1947 when the Norwegian Thor Heyerdahl floated his boat "Kon-Tiki" through Peru across the Pacific Ocean to Easter Island to show that it was possible that these islands could be inhabited through South Americans. This kind of archaeology style is well-known at Stonehenge due to the enormous technical issues that are being asked at the site. For instance, how did the stones travel to be shaped, transported, and then constructed?

At Stonehenge The experimental archaeologists have employed elaborate pulleys to lift replicas of the trilithons made of concrete tried to drag bluestones out of Wales and even tried to test the theory that the stones transported on massive stones "ball bearings."[11Although this is entertaining to watchand may sometimes prove the validity of different theories, archaeology that is experimental as it is currently conducted cannot be able to prove the method by which Stonehenge was constructed, just what it wasn't. Recently, archaeology research has been attempting to recreate the life of the builders, not just their methods of construction. It is the Neolithic Houses Project attempts to rebuild the houses that the builders lived in (based on archaeological findings at Durrington Wells, a nearby site) Wells) and also have interpreters on hand to attempt to carry out all the essential activities of life (cooking and making tools, farming, etc.) within the structures. This is a one of the aspects of the post-Childe shift in archaeology, away from stunning sites and towards the reconstruction of the lives of the ancient and communities.

The evolution of modern archaeology has played a huge role in shaping the current perception of the place. Chemical analysis has contributed to the increasing interest in re-creating prehistoric landscapes. The most well-known chemical analysis method is the carbon dating technique that makes application to analyze Carbon 14 residues in prehistoric organic matter to establish the precise date that the creature that was once living died however, it has also had many applications across archaeology. Modern archaeologists are more of a chemist than an excavator. The use of chemical dating has given archaeologists the previously unattainable Holy Grail: a precise time frame for the construction of historic structures and their activities.

A place as famous such as Stonehenge was perfect for dating using chemical methods however, the reality is that stones are not suitable for radiocarbon tests. Therefore, radiocarbon dating was applied only to the traces of residue that were discovered under Stonehenge in the year 1995. This was which was three years following the inception of the method. Along with additional research during 2008, archaeologists were capable of affixing the most precise date to Atkinson's chronology from 1979 which has pushed the construction date back to around 3000 BC. [14]

While the work, carried out mostly at the primary Stonehenge area, has attracted significant media attention[15] Other archaeologists have been striving to expand the concept to "Stonehenge" over the stone monuments to include the entire surroundings of the site, including the adjacent Stonehenge stone circles of Avebury. Although archaeologists have been involved in the surrounding area since for a long time, beginning with Gowland as well as Hawley's explorations of tombs around it however, it has been the subject of more attention in recent times due to various reasons.

Stone circle Avebury

Perhaps the most pressing problem is the poor condition of Stonehenge's condition. For a long time stonehenge's UN World Heritage Site authority archaeologists, archaeologists, and neo-pagan organizations have complained that the adjacent roads could harm the monument, and one is actually cutting through Stonehenge's processional avenue. In fact, English Heritage, the site's administrator, is now recognizing that some changes are required. [16]

View from the air of Stonehenge

This has led people who are interested to advocate for an accurate restoration that reflects the Neolithic landscape, however that will only create questions about how the Neolithic landscape was like. Modern archaeological techniques permit greater knowledge to be gained from the analysis of the ancient pollen and wood ash which allows archaeologists sketch the landscape that the builders sawas hardwood oak forests that were rich in game. These methods culminated in the closing decades in the second half of 20th century, with books such as Reconstructing Iron Age Societies: New Perspectives on The British Iron Age (1997) edited by Adam Gwilt and Colin Haselgrove in addition to Stonehenge in its Natural Landscape: Twentieth Century Excavations (1995) Edited by Rosamund M.J. Cleal, K.E. Walker as well as R. Montague. In addition, more recently the use of Global Positional Satellites (GPS) and mapping technology that is computer-generated like Geographic Information Systems (GIS) allow archaeologists to map out the sites' locations and then compare the various types of data to create map representations of the construction landscapes were like. [18]

The consensus is growing that the Stonehenge site as we are able to see it today was just the central point of what was considered to be the most important landscape for funerary purposes for the builders of it, such as the chapel that is at the center of an old cemetery. For instance in 2003-2008, the Stonehenge Riverside Project found that rituals of funerary were a major part of the Stonehenge site since its first version, and it could have served as the burial site for the most prominent and richest people. The work has resulted in the discovery of crucial sites in the area, including the neolithic village at Durrington Wallsand a third neolithic Stone and Wood henge that is about half a mile away from Stonehenge it self that was later discovered to be buried beneath the earth (and found by ground-penetrating radar),[21as well as another henge, dubbed "Bluestonehenge". Bluestonehenge is about one mile from Stonehenge in the Avenue which runs to Stonehenge on the solstice axis,[22and some archaeologists have claimed that this second Neolithic henge may be an old barrow. The discoveries and the ensuing discussions, all of which have been made in the past 10 years, indicate it is possible that the Stonehenge Landscape is only now getting better understood and that a deeper understanding of the area is likely to be gained through further study.

The excavations at Durrington Walls

Computer rendering of Bluestonehenge

Chapter 3: Folklore And History

The existence of Stonehenge on the Salisbury Plain has always been widely known in Britain and speculation about Stonehenge has always been a part of the location. One of the first written reports is Geoffrey of Monmouth's Historia Regum Britanniae (cir. 1136) ("History of the British Kings") that attributes the construction of the site in the hands of the magician Merlin. According to mythology, Merlin brought the stones across from Ireland via magic or through the aid of giants. The theories continued to be debated as the years passed, and one was proposed from the well-known designer Inigo Jones, one of his staff visited the area in 1655. Jones claimed that it was probably the site of a Roman temple. However, up to in the late 19th century Stonehenge did not receive much attention as more than a tourist attraction and was not considered a major pilgrimage or tourist destination.

The illustration in the 12th century shows a massive helping Merlin create Stonehenge.

It is the earliest documented illustration of Stonehenge in recorded history.

Despite these enigmatic legends and wild speculations The site's past going in time to Norman period is well-known because it's located within an area which was extensively cultivated over the course of decades. Stonehenge was first mentioned in the land tenure system in the form of an estate owned by Amesbury Abbey, then transferred during the Reformation to the Earl of Hartford. Stonehenge went through many different hands before coming into the Antrobus family, whose final heir passed away in World War I. Stonehenge was auctioned off by a local baronet , who donated it to the State.

Farm carts passing by Stonehenge in the 1880s.

Although Stonehenge is currently owned by the Crown but the state has seen several different organizations control the location. It is currently run through English Heritage, an appointed entity created in 1983 to oversee archaeological sites that are owned by the government. The rest of the area was picked by a nationwide fundraising campaign in the 1920s. It was then was given by the National Trust, an independent non-profit organization dedicated to the preservation of land. The Trust owns 827 hectares surrounding the site, and includes numerous smaller archeological sites. Therefore, unlike the nearby Avebury Circle, there has not been any significant settlements of modern times on or surrounding the site, meaning that the site has maintained its rural feel.

But it's not that Stonehenge was a secluded location. In the wake of the rising popularity of alternative religions like the counterculture, neo-paganism as well as that of the pop and rock culture, Stonehenge has continued to serve a purpose beyond as an "historic place" but also as a location in which modern events take place. Additionally, mythological stories continue to be abound about the site including people who attribute Stonehenge to work done by aliens that are based on written works of Erich von Daniken. Other people consider that Stonehenge is linked to the spiritual energy lines known as "Ley Lines" which cross Britain.

With all the mystery as well as the background as well as the arguments, it's not surprising that Stonehenge is among the most debated, decried and debated ancient site that exists currently. It is the only monument that has been questioned. crucial importance -- such as its purpose in the first place as well as its creators and their current meaning and the best way to ensure the preservation of its monument -- have been resolved with anything close to the level of scholarly consensus. Every year, it's the scene of an "annual solstice celebration of clash between the forces that are in order and disorder"[2727. A large part of this conflict is because the place is of immense significance in terms of spiritual and symbolic value for the vast majority of Druids, Neo-pagans, New Age Travellers, and other people belonging to the British "counterculture."

A photograph of a druid's ceremony of initiation at Stonehenge in 1905.

The tension is caused by it being the case that, for officials who are the guardians of and interpreters for Stonehenge (including English Heritage, the National Trust, English Nature and the archeological community Stonehenge is essentially a symbol that is a part of the past, and part of the British "heritage." But for those who belong to counterculture communities, Stonehenge is far from frozen and dead. It is, to quote the words of the cultural scholar Andy Worthington, a "living temple" and an "icon of alternative Britain".

The main focus of this battle was always the dramatic and visually stunning events that happen in the winter and summer solstices, particularly the dawn alignments on the summer solstice. many Britons have discovered to be the ideal moment for a celebration that lasts all night long of love and life. These customs, which were invented around the turn of the century are the result of a social and religious movement known as Druidism or as a contrast with the pre-Roman roots of Neo-Druidism.

"The Druid's (or Gorsedd) Prayer

Original written by Iolo Morganwg

This Version was composed by this Version is by the Order of Bards, Ovates and Druids

"Grant To the holy Ones, Thy Safety;

In the area of protection, strength;

In addition, in the strength of knowing;

In understanding, understanding;

In the realm of the realm of knowledge, in justice;

In the understanding of justice, and the desire for it;

In that love, that love of all beings;

In"the love that is everywhere in life forms that love for Earth our mother, and everything good."

Stonehenge and stone monuments of the same type throughout Britain are unquestionably associated in the minds of citizens from Britain to the "druids" from the time of the writings of archaeologist of the 18th century William Stukeley. Stukeley however, did not have all the answers; throughout Britain the higher class (often Anglican) Britons were looking to learn about the old "Celtic" religious traditions of their respective islands. Druids for many were a popular choice and they began to create Druidic Orders according to the works of scholars such as Stukeley along with Iolo Morganwg (1747-1826). Morganwg was an Iolo Morganwg, a Welsh nationalist was believed to have discovered documents detailing the rituals of the druids, and even though it's known that he falsified the original documents, his ceremonies have left a lasting impression on the current Druidic Movement. A variation of his ceremony is still held annually at Stonehenge.

The writings of writers like Morganwg was helped by the natural beauty of the place. The romantics of the 19th century were often lost in the Salisbury Plain's bleak, wild and windswept environment. They were the first to popularize the idea that"the "sublime," a natural landscape that could create terror of God in the viewer and was in contrast to the "beautiful" landscapes which represented the soft and pleasant nature. Visitors to the 19th century's Stonehenge were not there to ponder the historical facts but rather to be horrified by the barbarism of the early Britons and the utter horror of the structure of the landscape. For those who were unable to visit the Stonehenge site in person Stonehenge was also a popular destination through the art of Romantic artists such as J.M.W. Turner as well as John Constable, who depicted the bleak, haunting landscape. The experience was viewed as a deeply aesthetic and religious one and has helped provide the basis for the spiritual connection between the neo-druids as well as the monument. Although archaeologists of the past may have had this same view but today, it is a fundamentally differentiating the scientific and religious connections individuals have with the monument.

Constable's drawing depicts Stonehenge (1835)

Turner's drawing depicts Stonehenge (1828)

The modern druid community has split in two parts. On one hand, there's the Gorseddau ceremonies, which are institutions that are located in Wales, Cornwall and the continental region of Brittany which aim to showcase their regional Celtic culture and language (Welsh, Cornish and Breton in particular) in the context of annual ceremonies and awards. These events are the combination of an annual Masonic ceremony as well as The Celtic Oscars, and the queen's annual knighthood nominations. These events are usually linked to stone circles. In the case of Boscawen Un, for instance. very first Cornish Gorsedd (the singular of Gorseddau) was held in 1928 within the Boscawen Un stone circle. Boscawen Un, and the larger Welsh Gorseth now uses custom-built stone circles for its ceremonies. Morganwg's ceremonies consciously combined these circles, making these sacred grounds that only people who belong to the Gorsedd Bards, who had been initiated and druids were allowed to enter.

But, even though Stonehenge could have been the image Morganwg was thinking of in the 1780s, it's not situated in the typical Celtic country. It is situated within the highly English county Wiltshire which is why it is not the location of the traditional nationalist Gorsedd ceremony. Instead, it's been adopted by the second segment that is part of the Druid tradition, which is the spiritual neo-pagans. For them, the Celtic languages aren't crucial. They instead seek to revive the pre-Christian sun worshipping religion that was prevalent in the islands. Druidism as it is in this form is a very dualistic religion that contrasts the male sun and the moon's female counterpart, rationality with Irrationality with Dark. [29]

The annual ceremony held in Stonehenge during the solstice season is conducted through members of the Glastonbury Order of Druids and their political wing, known as the Loyal Arthurian Warband. Members of the order wear ceremonial robes and enter the circle. They follow a ritual that is that is based on Morganwg's original. They join an sacred circle, as they "call" for the directions of the 4 cardinal cards and blowing a ram's trumpet and chanting the ritual query "is the peace there?" The ritual is followed by the invocation of the Druid's prayer which was written by Morganwg and used by Gorseddau and Neo-Druids. the ceremony and prayers continue until the culmination: the sun rising upon the Heelstone. The druids will perform another ritual around noon, after which they declare the circle "opened" that is to say anyone who is not initiated can get to enter. From the time of the Free Festivals, the members from The New Age Traveller community enter and conduct marriages, baby ceremony of naming and scatter the ashes of their deceased and generally mingle to the stone and with one another. [30]

This ancient ritual (and the annual huge crowds) continued to be largely unchanged through the beginning into the century of 20th. But, in the 1970s there was an increase in interest in the Stonehenge site among people who were involved in alternate "New Age" faiths, and a lot of believed that it was the epitomized site of the ancient holy sites. Many of whom were branded "hippies" in the media began arriving at Stonehenge from the middle of the 1970s, and established an all-new tradition called Stonehenge Free Festival. Stonehenge free festival.

Tradition of the summer celebrations at Stonehenge is actually much more ancient in comparison to Stonehenge Free Festival. Stonehenge Free Festival which began the first festival recorded in 1680, and the first midsummer celebration in 1781. The 19th century was the time of struggle there were legal battles regarding the rights that the property owner had to enclose the site, as well as to charge for entry and to prohibit celebrations. It was the discovery of this alignment as well as the growth of neo-Druidry led to the fact that the place was used for religious celebrations by Druidic groups from the 1920s onwards. The druidic rituals inevitably was a crowd of curious spectators. [31]

The scene grew further in 1974-84 when the first The Free Festival, growing out of an New Age interest in the area. In the beginning, groups of wandering pagans started to set up camp in nearby fields and held an annual festival that culminated on the solstice. However, the celebrations grew in the size of. Then there was a gathering every year to form a national group made up of "New Age Travellers" who traveled around Britain in small groups. Apart from the religious aspect, Stonehenge became a central occasion on their calendar for the Travellers and offered the opportunity to meet as a group. It was an "free event," but there was no charge for admission and no authority to govern. As the historian and archaeologist Christopher Chippendale noted, it was an "time in which it was believed that the Lord of Misrule rules" and for them, it was more than "a unremarkable agnostic monument to be examined by archaeologists from the academic field, but an important place for living power". As early as 1978 the Travellers have criticized the custodians' management, including that there is a roadway which separates an avenue from the henge, the huge parking area that was paved as well as the decrepit visitor's facilities as well as the barbed wire and the arch lamps.

There was there was a rise in the use of drugs. In 1982, a street of tents was openly selling controlled substances at marked prices. In 1983, the festival was extended to six weeks and had a total of 30000 people. Naturally, the magnitude and duration of the event affected the surrounding countryside. In the in the same year, government joined various previous organizations including that of the Ancient Monuments Board for England as well as the Historic Buildings Council for England and the division for monuments of the Department of the Environment - to form an autonomous semi-autonomous English Heritage. The issue regarding what would become the Stonehenge Free Festival quickly became the first major issue for the organization as the newly appointed Commissioners were quick to respond.

Photo taken at Stonehenge Free Festival in 1984. Stonehenge Free Festival in 1984

In in 1985 English Heritage - supported by Wiltshire County Council - banned all gatherings, even ceremonies that are separate from Druidic ceremonies on the site. They distributed hundreds of signs, won the authority to shut down roads, and erected new razor wire restraints on the area. The proposals of Traveller groups to create alternative venues for festivals in the site were denied. This created the conditions for an event that would be regarded as the most significant occasion in the city's 20th century. [33]

The month of June, 1985 was the time that Margaret Thatcher's administration included the "exclusion zone" during the Summer Solstice for four miles across the entire circumference of Stonehenge and barred all visitors However, an assemblage of new age travelers referred to as "The Convoy" tried to contest an exclusion line. The Convoy was comprised of between 80-120 vehicles and more than 700 people. The convoy walked towards the henge in mass, but was blocked by mounds gravel that were piled up on the road. The procession that was stopped was confronted by the police, around 1,600 people had gathering for the celebration and used billy clubs to smash into windshields. The majority of the crowd fled to an adjacent beanfield, and they were attacked. The attempts to negotiate an escape were rejected by police and the result was a lengthy standoff resulted. During the standoff several Convoy members were beaten and removed, mostly with head injuries and a medical ambulance. As riot police arrived, Convoy members tried to flee , some even in their cars - but were pursued and assaulted by police. The events that followed are debated, however Convoy members say that the police attacked them with fire extinguishers, rocks and police riot equipment. In total, more than 700 Travellers were detained, the most significant arrests in British history until that time. [34]

Thatcher did not have a lot of affection for her fellow New Age Travellers, reportedly calling them "a group of medieval Brigands" as well as Both Thatcher along with Her predecessor (fellow Conservative John Major) attempted to restrict their movements. The government barred them from camping and monitored their movements and rounded them up throughout the countryside. However, research of Traveller populations showed that a lot were homeless or unemployed in 1985, as a direct consequence of the restructuring and deindustrialization of the

British economy. It seems that the crackdown in the Beanfield was just the beginning strike in a bigger campaign that aimed to criminalize their lifestyle, as well as any major protest or other gathering.

In the immediate post-Beanfield time there was a push to stress the necessity for "protect" Stonehenge. For example in 1985, the documentary "Who created Stonehenge?" for the BBC's show Horizon began with the following description: "It's a magnet for people from all over world. Every year, 34 of a million people travel to visit the site. They're willing to pay for the privilege of looking at a wreckage. To safeguard what's left however, they aren't allowed to go in and are held away. [...] in order to safeguard Stonehenge, over two years, the Neo-Druids are prohibited from hosting their ritual along with hippies who view Stonehenge as their sacred site of peace and love."

In 1997 the American documentary on PBS's PBS program NOVA (1997) offered an even more fervent stand: "In the 20th century the modern religion of Druids made the temple their own and made it an arena for elaborate solstice celebrations. In the 70s and 80s, their pagan worship was gradually taken over by hippies, drug use and the media from around the world. To preserve Stonehenge, British authorities now close Stonehenge during the summer solstice."

Today, the solstice festivities once again draw hundreds of spectators. The events have seen attendance of up to 14,500 (in the year 2012) in 2012 and 18,000 (2011) despite the rain during both days. There is certain to be a religious element present as well, with revelers pushing their bodies against the stones to soak in their healing energy and others participating in extravagant Druidic ceremonies (including two weddings in 2011) The majority of the event could be described as an emotional joyful celebration. The festivities are filled with colorful costumes with feathers, floral arrangements, and a bizarre musical ensemble (for example the jam session that is consisting of conga drummers tuba, flute, and the horn of a ram). The Body of the Peace Convoy might have been destroyed however, the spirit which animates the

Travellers during the 1970s and 1980s remains.

One of the spirits that move and a symbol of the current culture circling around the stones is Arthur Uther. Formerly known as John Rothwell, Pendragon (born in the year 1958) was an active participant in the Free Festivals that predated Beanfield as part of a motorcycle band. He officially changed his name in 1986, shortly following Thatcher's suppression of the Free Festivals. Along with the political section of the Glastonbury Order of Druids, became the center of stone-related protests, by taking part in and providing the most magical support for environmental protests throughout Britain. Their biggest victory came when Pendragon contests the English Heritage prohibition on Solstice celebrations at the European Court of Human Rights one time in 1998 and in 2009. [39]

The 20th century's events at Stonehenge also led to changes inside the Neo-Druidic community. The old druidry was often associated with the elderly Anglicans as well as Celtic nationalists. However, the new

Druidry was able to accept the appeal of the Free Festival and the "Lord of Misrule." Organisations such as those of the Secular Order of Druids, the Loyal Arthurian Warband and the Glastonbury Order of Druids were established in the latter half of the 1980s to contest the actions of the government which led to an increase in the Beanfield: English Heritage, the police and The County Government and the Conservative Government's Powers-that be in Parliament. They evolved into protest groups, making use of the battle for Stonehenge as an important rallying point and a gauge to their larger movements for environmental protection and nuclear disarmament as well as the return to what they see as the pre-Christian ideals. In the present they remain prominent participants of the British Druid community.)

Chapter 4: The Tourism And Context

Most people think that Stonehenge is not a site of research in the academic sense nor an object of worship. For the majority of people, it's an historic place and an attractive tourist destination. Over the years thousands of people have trekked across the Salisbury Plain each year, which has made Stonehenge an extremely sought-after places in Britain.

Despite its remoteness, Stonehenge is a relatively accessible place for visitors to explore and it is extremely loved. Visitors typically travel via car, commuting along the A3028 west of Andover as well as eastbound from Warminster. There is parking available at the site, but visitors are also able to access public transport using to the Salisbury train station or the local buses that go to the site. For those who are more adventurous, they can use to use the National Cycle Network or hike for just a two-mile stroll from Amesbury.

A lot of visitors today experience mixed reactions to the monument, something most experts (including English Heritage) recognize. It's certainly an impressive landmark, however it is located on the road A344 which is a cut across the top of the sacred Avenue (where sunlight sets on the solstice of summer) and is almost as the A304. Many people are stunned at the sight of the site coming to their attention while driving and are usually put off by the lack of fencing around the perimeter. The visitor's center is also disappointing. A decrepit 1960s prefabricated structure that connects to a concrete tunnel underneath the A344 before reaching the Stonehenge site. It is also clear that even though everyone is aware of a bit about Stonehenge but many are amazed by the fact that the site isn't much bigger than they thought it would be.

However there are some positive shifts taking place. After years of complaints by archaeologists, heritage officials, the druid community and uncounted tourists, English Heritage has launched plans for 2013-14 to complete the renovation of the site. The plan, with an estimated amount that is PS27 million, will see removal of the A344 and the building of a visitor center and the conversion thousands of hectares surrounding land into chalk plains that are not fenced that resemble the neolithic landscape. It is also planned to create a recreation of a village that was neolithic-era, that is based on archaeological excavations nearby and allow visitors to walk by the Avenue, just in the way that was planned by the construction workers thousands of years ago. Many believe that the plans aren't coming quickly enough, given that there is growing agreement that Stonehenge is the jewel in the crown in British Heritage, is one of the most embarrassing things that Britain has ever endured. [42]

For those who can't go to the first Stonehenge it is not lost as Stonehenge has reached the position of an authentic worldwide icon. It is immediately recognizable, and has been cited, copied and mocked thousands of times. The mere sight of it evokes thoughts about the past rituals, druidic rites and Neolithic creativity. This is why Stonehenge is a symbol that can be that is adapted to different contexts. The most entertaining of these are the fake henges: Carhenge (a replica built in the

Nebraska cornfields made of the old Buicks that was built in the year the year 1987), Foamhenge (a "perfect" replica constructed from foam from Virginia), Twinkiehenge (built during in 2001 at the Burning Man Festival out of the popular ready-to-eat food), Tankhenge (in post-Berlin Wall Berlin, made from Soviet transporters for personnel) and an unidentified replica of the popular street artist Banksy built using portable toilets in 2007's Glastonbury Festival. Also, there's the Stonehenge and astronomical references: Manhattanhenge (the name for the day that the sun sets or rises across the east-west avenues of Manhattan in a similar way to what it happens through the stones that make up the stone stones of the) in addition to MITHenge (a identical phenomenon in an extensive hallway at the Massachusetts Institute of Technology). The Stonehenge phenomenon has even been used in the scene of heavy metal due to Black Sabbath and their tour with a replica from 1983 to and Stonehenge gave its name to the World War II submarine that went missing in the Pacific in 1943.

It's no doubt there is no doubt that Stonehenge is the most important megalithic site that exists in Britain and that its surroundings could become one of the most well-preserved evidences of Britain's Neolithic people. Megalithic structures are not exclusive only to Stonehenge as well as Britain It is characteristic of the whole Atlantic Coast of Europe, and similar structures are found in different parts of the world. The European megalithic culture built many types of structures: From Irish courts tombs, to Cornish quoits mesolithic tombs in Scandinavia or even those of the Skorba burial sites of Malta. Beyond Europe the same traditions are found in locations that are as dispersed such as Easter Island, Northern China and Yemen.

Outside of Stonehenge Perhaps the most well-known and significant megalithic monument is the henge located at Avebury. The site is just 20 miles away from Stonehenge It was built from similar sarsens and existed prior to Stonehenge's more well-known stonehenge. Avebury is unique for its size, being the biggest circular stone in Britain with over 1,000 feet in circumference. The community of Avebury was constructed into the circle, and sometimes and incorporating the rough-hewn stone into the walls of houses. Similar to Stonehenge It also features the "avenue" of the approach (the "Kennet Avenue") and a number of other sites nearby: it is also home to the West Kennet Long Barrow and Silbury Hill, a 125 feet high artificial hill both of which date back to Avebury itself. Avebury is well-loved by many tourists due to the lack of restrictions surrounding the area. Visitors can walk among the stones and touch them, leave offerings, and take photos.

Avebury Henge and Village

The phenomenon of the stone circle known as the "Henge" can be all over Britain. The term "Henge" originates from Stonehenge and was later retroactively applied to similar structures in other locations. Some of the more well-known places include The Thornborough Henges in Yorkshire, comprised of three identical Henges that are aligned in a row as well as The Ring of Brodgar on the island of Orkney as well as

Boscawen-un in Cornwall, as well as Boscawen-un and The Merry Maidens (two circular structures within view of each other) within Cornwall.

An aerial view of Thornborough's 3 Henges

Brittany which is now a region under the control of France is a long-standing region that has significant cultural connections to the Celtic people from southern Britain and hosts many megaliths. Among them is one called the Broken Menhir from Er Grah at the village of Locmariaquer. It was the biggest stone built by prehistoric peoples. It stood at over 60 feet high and weighing 254 tonnes. To put it in perspective, Stonehenge used sarsen stones which were smaller than 25 tons and 12 feet to make up the outer circle, and twenty feet to make up The Great Trilithon. Over a lengthy period of space and time, these sites were probably constructed by different groups of cultures and have the same architectural history, and possibly theological reasons. At present, the reason and the history of each remain a mystery.

The Broken Menhir of Er Grah

Outside of Europe There are many wealthy Megalithic tradition. It is the Near East is home to megalithic tombs and standing stones in a large area, that extends north from Yemen across Jordan, Syria, Israel, Lebanon and Turkey. The most densely populated area with standing stones can be found in the Golan Heights, which lie along the border between Israel as well as Syria. A different large-stone tradition existed in the present northeastern China as well as in the Korean Peninsula. Further to the south, a megalithic culture existed in a few regions of Indonesia up to the 20th century particularly around the island of Nias. Some believe that the well-known Moai statues from Easter Island should be considered megaliths since they definitely fit the criteria for their size. The Moai specifically have inspired the same amount of mystery and experimentation in archaeology as Stonehenge and Stonehenge, with the same debates on the what, when what, why and who built them.

Chapter 5: Intrigue And Mystery

If you mention Stonehenge and a lot of people immediately visualize an ancient structure that has a religious significance. They imagine pictures of Druids at dawn, the solstices of winter and summer as well as celebrations.

There are a myriad of old circles scattered throughout the UK which is estimated to be of 900 at present and possibly 4,500 at some point. The first ones were made out of wood, but they transformed to stone during the latter part of the Neolithic and the early Bronze Age period. Stonehenge could, therefore, be considered to be just one among many.

However, it is certainly distinctive. It's an incredible engineering feat, particularly when you consider that it was created by people with only the most basic tools to complete the task. Its story spans 4500 years, which is longer that the Egyptian pyramids and perhaps even longer and there is evidence of significant constructions at the site dating further back two hundred years. In fact, several large Mesolithic postholes discovered beneath the present car park are believed to date back to 8000 BC which suggests a 10,000-year plus use of the site.

Stonehenge is situated within the County of Wiltshire just 2 miles west of Amesbury and Salisbury around eight miles further north. Stonehenge is considered to be the most important historic monument within the UK and is legally protected as it is a Scheduled Ancient Monument since 1882.

The first time that we have written about Stonehenge occurred in the Twelfth Century , when the historian and the explorer Henry of Huntingdon identified the characteristics of Stonehenges. At the time the man was making speculations about the reasons why and how it was constructed. In later writing, he called the monument "Stanhenge," "Stonhenge", and the 'stone hisgles' and, finally, in 1610, Stonehenge as we know it now.

The term "henge" generally is a reference to an earthwork dating back to that of the

Neolithic period. The name Stonehenge could, therefore, is derived from the expansion of the site, when standing stones were added on top of the original earthwork. Additionally, references are made to hanging stones' or'supported stones' to support the name, and others mention that the lintels "hinge" on stone uprights.

The Stonehenge Project is changing ownership Stonehenge

The king Henry VIII acquired Amesbury Abbey and the surrounding land, which included Stonehenge however ownership has changed several times since. The estate was transferred to the Earl of Hertford in 1540. He later transferred it to the Lord Carleton. From him, it passed into the hands of the Marquis of Queensbury and in 1824, it was purchased from the Antrobus family from Cheshire.

The last heir to the family died in World War I, Stonehenge and the surrounding land was auctioned off on the 21 September 1915. The property was purchased for the sum of

$6,600 from Cecil Chubb, apparently as an impulse because he believed Stonehenge should be local owned by the local community. He gave Stonehenge in the following years to government officials, under the conditions that it be taken care of properly and open to the public for visits. He was knighted for it.

In the 1920s, the construction of modern structures within the immediate area was threatened Stonehenge and a massive call was made to preserve the site. The results of the appeal allowed the land surrounding it to be purchased and donated to the National Trust, which removed the structures and restored the land to agriculture. This is taking a step further and the land is being converted to open grassland in the same way as it was prior to when Stonehenge was constructed.

Stonehenge is currently part of the Crown and is managed through English Heritage. The land around it is managed and owned through The National Trust. National Trust.

Controversies and questions linger On

About 3,500 years later, the building of Stonehenge ended and, after a lengthy time of degradation over the years finally seemed that Stonehenge was secure to be used in the near future. There are, however, questions about how the landscape and site is maintained and managed and the inevitable issues which have plagued Stonehenge for years.

Despite all the studies conducted and the millions of pages written on Stonehenge there are many questions and not enough answers remain. What was the reason and how it was constructed? What was the purpose behind it? What is the reason, even after all these years, is it still the attention of millions of people?

While some of these questions have been addressed to some extent however, there are many contradicting theories and the jury's not yet in place in a large number of cases. This does contribute to the mystery that is a part of Stonehenge which will continue to keep archaeologists and scientists engaged for years to be.

Stonehenge is a stunning sight that dominates the landscape. It's an awe-inspiring creation, made by thousands of people working in conjunction with primitive equipment and techniques. Despite the impressive nature their accomplishment the spiritual and inspiring ambience of the area remains the most prominent impression.

The Site Today's Features Site Today

The central feature that makes up Stonehenge is the Stone Circle, which consists of several standing stones with some having stone lintels. Around these stones is the circular earth bank and ditch that are believed to be the product from the very beginning phases of construction in this area.

The stone circle is made up of an inner and an outer set of stones. These are stone sarsen (a kind of sandstone) with the average of weight 25 tons , or the bluestones with a smaller weight which weigh between two and five tons per. While the bluestones aren't actually blue, they are an eerie blue hue when they are they are wet. They have 83 stone altogether.

The sarsens were built in the form of an inner horseshoe with an outer circle. The horseshoe consists of 5 trilithons (two vertical stones, with an horizontal lintel at the top) Of which two are partially ruined, and three remain. One of them was destroyed in 1797, but restored in the year 1958. A stone that fell from the trilithon with the highest height obscures it. Altar Stone, which is located in the middle of the horseshoe.

The trilithons' stone fragments are the biggest of them all, with a weight of up to fifty tonnes each. They are laid out in a symmetrical fashion and joined by a complex joining. Some stones feature carvings of axe heads as well as daggers that are believed as Bronze Age weapons.

The outer circle is surrounded by the horseshoe. It was originally made up of thirty sarsen stones, each capped with lintels. However, many pieces have fallen, and certain lintels and stones are missing.

Only 17 of the sarsen stones remain, and each measures 13 inches (4.1 metres) tall and 6 feet 11 inches (2.1 metres) tall and 2.1 metres wide.

Some of the sarsen stones fell to the ground during Roman rule of Britain and three were destroyed in 1797, and two more fell in the year 1900, with the last five stones were reconstructed in the year 1958. In the sarsens is an inner oval and a circle made up of bluestones. Some have been blown away, while others are gone and many are simply stumps.

A single of the important characteristics of the stones, that create Stonehenge distinctive in its design is the way in which they were joined. Lintels were attached to the standing stones by using mortise holes and protruding Tenons as their lintels joined with groove and tongue joints typically utilized in woodworking.

The Surrounding Bank and Ditch

Around the stones is the earth banks that are circular in shape as well as a ditch which surrounded the area. To the east of the north is the principal entrance, with one smaller entrance in the south. There are many gaps in the present due to later tracks being built throughout the area.

The Avenue is a 12-metre-wide area, which is now marked with low bank, is the entry point with the River Avon. The main entrance's outside are an entrance to the Heel Stone, a large slab of sarsen that is unshaped and the largest in all time at approximately thirty tonnes. It originally had an adjacent stone. If you are within the inner circle during the summer solstice can observe the sun rising above this Heel Stone.

Nearby There is also close to the entrance is the Slaughter Stone, 16 feet (4.9 meters) long and now a smoldering ruin it was named that way due to the belief that it could be utilized as a location to perform human sacrifice. There were four Station Stones, only two of them remain, were used to mark the edges of a rectangle and are believed to be related to the solstice axis or the original setting that was created by Stonehenge.

In the enclosure there are 56 pits named the 'Aubrey Holes', named after John Aubrey who first discovered them in the latter part of the Seventeenth Century. The majority of them were discovered to be burial sites for cremation which is a sign of the first burial ground There are also suggestions the holes were created to serve as a base for a bluestone standing circle.

The most recent enhancements made to Stonehenge site, completed in 2014, were replica Neolithic houses that were constructed in the vicinity of the visitor centre. These replicas were constructed with authentic materials and techniques with dung and wattle walls that are topped with high pitched thatched roofs. They were intended to demonstrate the visitors what life was like 4500 years ago, but are not universally embraced which has led to the controversy that has surrounded Stonehenge.

Chapter 6: Importance Of Stonehenge

Stonehenge's special location as a prehistoric landmark important site was acknowledged when it was given, in the year 1986, alongside the nearby Avebury, World Heritage status. Stonehenge was one of the first places located in the UK to be added to the UNESCO World Heritage list.

The award comes with an World Heritage Site Management Plan which outlines the significance of the site. It states:

"The Stonehenge, Avebury, and Associated Sites World Heritage Site is globally renowned because of its impressive complexes of ancient monuments. Stonehenge has the distinction of being the world's most sophisticated architecturally-designed prehistoric stone circle anywhere in the world, and Avebury is the biggest of its kind in all the planet. Together with the inter-connected monuments and the surrounding landscapes, they assist us in understanding Neolithic as well as Bronze Age ceremonial and mortuary practices. They show around 2000 years of continuous use as well as construction of monuments between. 3700 to 1600 BC. In this way, they are an exceptional representation of our shared heritage."

Its significance stems from several factors that include the immense difficulties involved when it came to transporting the materials , their construction and the advanced techniques employed. It is still the only remaining stone circle that was lintelled anywhere in the world, and was among the largest cemeteries for cremation in Neolithic Britain during the initial phases of its development. It's also situated in an area with numerous burial mounds, monuments, and monuments dating back to early in the Neolithic as well as the Bronze Age period, so it's a crucial archeological feature of that time.

The significance and fame of any significant site is often evaluated by the amount of variations available around the world. For instance, in the instance of Stonehenge there exist replicas of the monument of the monument in Australia as well as New Zealand, a World War I memorial in

Washington State that resembles the stone, and even a "Carhenge" in Nebraska in which cars have been erected instead of stones.

The lessons to be learned

Stonehenge and its surrounding sites offer vital information on the evolution of archaeology as well as the way people lived their lives and the way society was organized in the past. Even now, it plays been used as a site that is sacred and has a importance to the culture, and remains a place for celebrations and celebrations.

Research and excavations continue to be conducted and have greatly improved our understanding of the reason and how Stonehenge was built and the way it was utilized. The development of new techniques has accelerated the process of understanding of Stonehenge and will ensure that the knowledge continues to expand and develop.

How Stonehenge Was Developed

Due to the size and complexity of the site and the absence of advanced techniques and tools at the time of its construction, Stonehenge continues to be thought of as a masterpiece of engineering. People who first studied the site were initially confused as to how given the resources at hand, Neolithic people could transport the stones, form and even erect them with this size.

The most important assets were the inventiveness of the architects and the sheer amount of manpower available as a unit to complete the task. This job took several hundred years, beginning with the initial construction believed to have been completed at around 3000 BC and completion in 1600 BC or later.

However, there is evidence that construction began earlier, thanks to post holes being discovered dating back to the year 8000 BC. A causewayed enclosure situated at Robin Hood's Ball, and Stonehenge Cursus (a length of parallel banks, with ditches on the outside) were both built around 2300 feet (700 metres) north of the site around 3500 BC.

It is widely believed that the beginning of the primary construction phase for Stonehenge was about 3000 BC and continued to be completed until 1500 BC which was a total of 1500 years. According to one estimate, around 30-million hours work was required in order to transport, extract form and erect the stones.

The Stonehenge site has been blamed on the Romans as well as the Danes as well as the Mycenae people of the Aegean Sea region, and many others The most commonly accepted idea is Stonehenge was constructed by the Druids which was a priestly group of Celts who maintained the legend about the Celts and conducted their religious ceremonies. But this doesn't match with the date of the stone's construction, and therefore the name for the builder remains a bit of unknown to the present.

It is First Phase of Development

The initial major advancement, which took place in 3000 BC was the building in 3000 BC of the enclosure for circular earthwork. A ditch was dug with tools made of antlers and the chalk which was excavated was used to construct the outer and inner banks. While the ditch was not continuous, it was constructed in sections, indicating that distinct groups were responsible for each section.

Oxen and deer bones as well as some flint tools were discovered in near the end of the ditch. They were well taken care of and more ancient than the antlers employed to construct the ditch. It is thought that they may be buried deliberately to signal the conclusion of an era, and to signal a change in trend of the development.

The structure was around 360 feet (110 meters) in length, with the ditch being six feet (two meters) deep. It was situated in grassland open to the air that slopped to a slight slope. Its main entry point was located to the east of the north, and an additional entrance towards the south. the earthworks encapsulated the so-called "Aubrey Holes'.

An excavation conducted in 2013 by professor Mike Parker Pearson, discovered the remains of 63 people within only one hole. The bones were discovered following an earlier excavation that took place in 1920. It discovered them inside the Aubrey Holes and relocated them. They were evidence of the usage for Stonehenge for burial place during a period of five centuries between 3000 BC until 2500 BC.

The outside bank of the earthworks has been largely taken away by the plough through the decades. The ditch and the inner bank remain and can be seen through the grass, as earthwork low in the ground.

The Site is being transformed

The next significant change on the area was construction of stone circles which took place around 2500 BC. It was an important development as it was a total shift in the construction materials between stone and wood. When compared to the construction of earthworks, this was a huge undertaking as it involved the source as well as the movement, preparation and erection of huge stones.

It is generally accepted that the bigger sarsen stone originate out of the

Marlborough Downs, about twenty miles away, and where huge quantities of these stones may still be seen. The smaller bluestones are found in a much more distant area and are attributed to those from the Preseli Hills in south-west Wales believed as being the primary source. The massive Altar Stone has been believed to originate out of The Brecon Beacons in South Wales.

A bluestone quarry located at Craig Rhos-y-felin in Pembrokeshire has been identified as being the possible stone's source. The quarry is about 150 miles (240 kilometers) away from Stonehenge and could have caused enormous logistical difficulties in transporting the stones that weigh a lot across this distance.

The task of transporting the Stones

One theory, as formulated by a group of Welsh researchers suggests it is that these stones were transported naturally by glaciers around 500 000 years ago. They believe that the holes made into the rock face of the Preseli Hills quarry, which claim to match the stones found at Stonehenge but are actually an organic formation, or could have been the result of archeological activities.

Another idea, put forth by professor Mike Parker Pearson, is that Stonehenge is the result of the site of a monument originally built in Wales before being relocated to its current location several years later. The evidence presented to support this is radiocarbon dating of the pits in the rock that suggest they were constructed between 300 and 500 years prior to when Stonehenge was constructed, as well as the evidence that the bone fragments that were discovered at Stonehenge seem to originate from people who came in the western part of Britain or possibly Wales.

It is believed that the bluestones of Stonehenge could be identified with the rock face in the quarry located in the Preseli Hills, and a excavation is planned to locate the site of the initial Welsh tomb. A small amount of research indicates that these stones may have been removed from the quarry several years prior to when

Stonehenge was constructed, which adds evidence to the notion that they were used first elsewhere.

Professor Pearson believes that the relocation in the memorial was because of a plan to move from Wales to create a base further to the east, possibly as an effort to bring together tribal warring groups. This involved not just moving individuals and their belongings but also the physical manifestation of their ancestors' ancestors in the shape of their remains as well as the burial site in which they were buried. If this is so it implies that the Neolithic society's religion and culture was based on the worship of those who were their predecessors.

How the Stones were obtained and moved

The most well-known theory is that bluestones were extracted from Quarry in Wales and later transported to Stonehenge. The extraction process involved putting wooden wedges into the cracks in the pillars then letting the rain expand the wood and break the stone, allowing it to be removed.

The move to Wales could have taken a lengthy and arduous process, involving sections of land and water. The first step could have been Milford Haven, where the stones were loaded on rafts. Then, the stones could be transported across south along the South Wales coast before coming across to the River Avon and the River Frome. Then, they could be dragged across the land until they reached a point close to Warminster in Wiltshire which is where they could have climbed back on rafts and transported across the River Wye to Salisbury, and then on through the River Avon to West Amesbury.

Instead of an straight line of just 150 miles This road would be around 24 miles. The movement of the stones across the land could be on sledges, or rollers. A 1995 experiment was a team of one hundred carrying a 40-ton slab 18 miles using an sleight that was running on a track that was greased with animal fat, which proved that the method of transportation could be a possibility.

It has been suggested that 500 men wearing ropes made of leather could be needed to lift one stone, while another 100 people were needed to place the rollers in front on the sledge. In addition, it has been suggested that oxen teams could be used to transport the stones.

The sarsen stones were likely to be dragged from the location using sledges or rollers and, though the distance was much shorter however, the weight was several times more. Another option would have been to place some stones on poles or frames and poles, which could be feasible for smaller stones which could weigh between two and two tons however not for the huge standing stones.

Making and erecting the Stones

After arriving on the site the stones needed been shaped into the correct shape with the hammer stones. Large hammerstones were used to break up portions of the stone, and smaller ones provided smooth finishes on the stone's surface. The stones weren't all completed to the same standard that was the case with those on the north east face and the sides of central trilithons more delicately finished.

A variety of broken hammerstones as well as large quantities of waste material from bluestones and sarsen stones were discovered in fields that lie to North of Stonehenge. This suggests that the stone's shaping was done there, and casts doubt on the notion of the stone being initially built elsewhere and later movedelsewhere, and other speculations that are more bizarre.

The final step was to put the stones in their final positions. This was a gruelling task. The best method is to dig a huge hole that had a slope in the front and an array of wooden stakes to the rear. The stone could then be taken into the hole most likely by using an A-frame made of wood and ropes made of plant fibre.

Additionally, weights might have been used to lift stones into an upright place. Once they were in the correct position the stones are supported by filling every hole in the ground with rubble.

Each stone that was placed on the ground is likely to have a tenon-carved on the top, while the lintel which was to be put on it would feature a mortise cut that had to need to precisely cut, shaped and cut to guarantee an ideal fitting. Each lintel was designed by curving the outside edge, to ensure that a circle was made.

The lintels would have likely been lifted on the stones by the aid of wooden platforms. Studies have revealed that it was possible to move the lintels on ramps with levers to move stones and timbers , which would have held them in place until the lintels made it to timber platforms , and then be pulled to their final location.

It was the groove and tongue joints which joined the lintels and mortise and tenon joints had to be precisely cut in order for them to ensure that they fit. Evidence of these joints are still visible today on a few pieces of stone.

The most recent discovery at Stonehenge believed to have occurred between the years 1600 to 1500 BC is the excavation of a pit ring known as Y holes. These are surrounded by another set of pits, referred to as Z holes, which surround the sarsen stones . They were dug a bit earlier. The reason for each pit is unclear.

While the Stonehenge that we are seeing today isn't like the one constructed over 3500 years ago the fact that much remains of it is an indication of the ability and perseverance of the builders who constructed it. A large portion of their work remains visible and remains an inspiration for those who visit it.

Chapter 7: Stonehenge's Purpose

The question of how Stonehenge was constructed has intrigued individuals for centuries now, motivations behind its construction have also been the same source of speculation. It is generally believed that one of its earliest purposes was to be burial grounds due to the abundance of cremated remains discovered at the site.

Stonehenge is believed as the biggest cemetery in Britain in the third millennium. burials taking place over a period of 500 years between 3000 BC between 2500 and 3000 BC. There are some experts who believe that the deceased were transported across the River Severn and then carried to Stonehenge most likely along the Stonehenge Avenue in an elaborate procession prior to cremation and burial.

Was Stonehenge a domain of the Dead?

One theory, offered from the professor Mike Parker Pearson, is that Stonehenge was a residence of the dead while close by Durrington Walls was a place for the living.

The deceased were transported in a ritual between life and death from the avenue of Durrington Walls to the River Avon and then back to the River Avon to Stonehenge by another route. This is in line with the findings on both sites, and stone henges are sometimes described as stone gallows as they were believed to mark the end of the world and were an entrance for humans to return to their roots.

Although burial is thought as the first usage of the site, it's not the main reason behind the site and a variety of theories continue to be debated. One of the major issues is the fact that the builders of the monument didn't leave any documents, and therefore theories can only be formulated through excavations and studies.

One theory that corresponds to the vast number of burials , and also an assumption that certain of those dead were believed to have suffered from trauma deformities one theory could be it believed that Stonehenge was a site of healing. This idea was proposed by professor Geoffrey Wainwright, president of the Society of

Antiquaries, and Timothy Darvill of Bournemouth University who believe that Stonehenge may be the earliest version of Lourdes in the present. The weight of this theory by the research that suggests that some of the remains that were discovered at Stonehenge were from different regions of Europe.

Then, an Observatory, Concert Hall or Something Else?

The stone's alignment with the open ends of the horseshoe-shaped stones aligned with the peaks of sunrise on the summer solstice as well as sunset at the winter solstice, have caused many to believe that Stonehenge was built to be an early type of observatory. It could have also allowed people to monitor and predict every equinox as well as other celestial events , such as moon eclipses. These were vital for their religious purposes.

This is the reason why this explanation is most favored by English Heritage, the site's operator, who states that Stonehenge is probably an ancient temple that was aligned with the movement of the sun. One hypothesis put forth in the work of Geoffrey of Monmouth in the 12th century is that Stonehenge was constructed as a memorial to the thousands of Britons who were killed in battle by Saxons.

Alongside the stones' alignment to the midsummer sunrise as well as Midwinter's sunset Stonehenge has also been said to be an exact geometric structure. Every aspect of the stones including size, weight, orientation and scope as well as distance are thought to be mathematically designed and demonstrate a thorough understanding of the geometry. Some believe that Stonehenge was designed with math in the mind of the creators.

Another idea, put forward by various researchers suggests that Stonehenge was a type of the early concert hall. This is based on reality that the stones, because of their size and shape, provide excellent acoustics, by amplifying the sounds of voices and music. Also, rubbing the stones has been proven to create an intense clanging sound.

The acoustic properties of these stones are, naturally be more than beneficial in the execution of rituals. They could also help clarify the reason why bluestones were transported to be used in the constructionprocess, since it was believed that they could have been taken from the vicinity of Maenclochog in Wales the name translates to "ringing rock" in Welsh and is the basis for their acoustic qualities. Bluestones were believed by many to possess healing properties, which goes along with the idea the idea that Stonehenge was a site of healing.

Ceremonial or Unification Goal

There are theories that Stonehenge may be a place of worship in which Danish monarchs were crowned, or that ancient alien visitors built models for the solar system at Stonehenge. It could also be there was a focus of an exercise designed to bring people to one another.

Stonehenge was constructed during a period when the Neolithic people of Britain were experiencing increased unity and therefore the construction was designed to display the unity of this group, as it required the cooperative efforts of a lot of people across long distances over an extended period. People at the time were believed to be in a state of cultural unity, and Stonehenge could have been constructed to symbolize the unification process.

A site that draws the attention of so many people for so long can not be noticed by extraterrestrial conspiracy theorists. Stonehenge is not an exception. It is believed to have been an encampment for aliens from space during the ancient times. In fact, there have been numerous reports of UFOs appearing close to the monument.

While excluding the more bizarre claims There is a consensus that Stonehenge was used for a variety of purposes during its long existence. It is likely that the burial ground was connected with religious ceremonies, which were also connected to the movements of the sun and the other planets.

The Solstice and other religious festivals

Whatever Stonehenge's origins and motives, the one thing that cannot be doubt is that the structure is in line with the movements of the sun, and it appears highly likely that this isn't a coincident.

The major elements of the monument -- the horseshoe-shaped formation of the five trilithons as well as The Heal Stone as well as the Avenue that connects towards River Avon River Avon -- are aligned with the sun rising on the summer solstice, and the sunset of winter solstice. In the year 2004, two massive pits were found within the South Cursus that are also aligned with midsummer's sunset and sunrise direction from to the Heel Stone.

The sunrise in midsummer comes from the north-east direction and is almost directly over the Heel Stone. In contrast, the sunset in mid-winter occurs located in the south-west region, within the space between two tallest trilithons, even though one of them is no more standing. The entrance from the north east that was widening around the year 2600 BC in the year 2600 BC when standing stones were built exactly matches the mid-summer sun and the sunset during mid-winter.

The significance of Solstices

Solstice's name originates from the word'solstitium"' which is which is a Latin word meaning the halting of the movement that the sun makes. The solstice in summer, typically at 21st July in the Northern Hemisphere signifies the time when the sun's elongated point to the north and is an extremely long day with daylight times exceeding 16.5 hours across the UK.

The winter solstice however is the day with the lowest degree of the year, typically 21st of December, when the sun begins to move towards the north. The equinoxes of autumn and spring are the dates between these two dates, usually 21st March and 21st Sept and are the dates that the sun has risen directly above the equator during its journey either north or south.

The most significant of these dates for different religious groups is the solstice of summer. For pagans, particularly it is the time to celebrate an ecumenical union between their God and Goddess. It also was used as a mark upon which the cultivation and harvesting of crops was planned.

The solstice of summer at Stonehenge is primarily connected to Druids who gather in large numbers just before the dawn of each year to celebrate the day. It became a popular event in the Twentieth century, when neo-Druids and other people who adhered to New Age beliefs began to frequently refer to Stonehenge as a site of significant religious significance.

In August 1905 The Ancient Order of Druids held an initiation mass at the temple, allowing more than 259 newly-initiated members of the Order. This ceremony received a lot of mocked during the time because of the fake beards of the participants and flowing white gowns. The drinking of large amounts of alcohol among the roughly 700 participants didn't help in portraying the ceremony as a serious affair.

There is Stonehenge Free Festival and the Battle of the Beanfield

The popularity of the rituals celebrated on the solstice of summer grew from 1972 until 1984 which was when it was the time that Stonehenge Free Festival was held. The event was attended by a growing number of revelers, at least 30,000 people in the final year who enjoyed the longest day of the year.

Stonehenge Free Festival ended in 1984. Stonehenge Free Festival ended after 1984 because the site was being closed to revelers in 1984 by English Heritage and the National Trust partially because of the pressure from local landowners concerned about the unruly behavior. However, on the solstice of summer in 1985, a number from New Age travellers and others who attended a variety of festivals as part of an ensemble called the Convoy wanted to go to Stonehenge the same way as previous years to host the event.

With the assistance of police helicopters The Convoy was tracked down to the bean field located in Wiltshire. The partygoers were reprimanded by riot police in order to stop from entering the Stonehenge site. The violence was widely referred to by the name of the Battle of the Beanfield.

In the past visitors to Stonehenge were allowed to stroll among the stones with no restrictions. This led to grave concerns over the damage and erosion, especially because of people climbing up on the stones. Thus, there were restrictions imposed through the roping of the stones to make them only seen from a small distance away.

Permits Limited Access

The stones are allowed with a special permit and is permitted during solstices in winter and summer. In the 15 years following the Battle of the Beanfield, there was no access to the stones. This meant that Druids were forced to conduct their festivities in front of the stones, on the edge of the road that was busy.

The situation changed at the close of the Twentieth Century, largely because of an organized campaign led by various Druid representatives as well as a campaigner referred to as the King Arthur Pendragon. It was the Court of Human Rights ruled that religious people can worship at their respective churches and, as neo-Druids Pagans, and others considered Stonehenge as their spot of worship, they ought to be permitted access.

In light of this ruling, only limited accessibility to stones is permitted four times per year, including solstices in winter and summer and also at the autumn and spring equinoxes. In the aftermath, the numbers are increasing at around of 30,000 in attendance during 2003, the year that summer solstice fell on the weekend.

Solstice celebrations aren't without the issues of modern-day life However. Due to a variety of terrorist attacks, police with guns are scheduled to be present on the festival grounds in order to increasing security level for all major festivals as well as other celebrations. Security measures that are expected to become a part of the festival in the near future, will also put restrictions on the size of bags and the search of festival-goers.

Other Monuments that have Similar Objectives

Stonehenge is not the only one in its significance in the celestial realm. There are a myriad of stone monuments throughout Britain. This includes the Scottish Callanish Stones on the Isle of Lewis and the Standing Stones of Stenness on the Isle of Orkney, which were constructed over five hundred years ago.

The research has revealed that the stones within the circles are placed in order in a way to align with the path of the moon and sun at various cyclic times. Along with their alignment with sunset and sunrise stones, the circles coincide with the northerly rising and the most southerly sunset of the moon. The arrangement of the stones is so that the stones are able to determine the lunar appearance at its northernmost location, which happens every 18.6 years.

They are believed to be significant to Neolithic people due to their religious beliefs. In order to do this they were capable of determining when days were beginning to get shorter and also when the sun was beginning its trek north, and when warmer weather was coming.

Because the structures are a bit less complicated than Stonehenge It is the goal to investigate them first, in order to uncover the secrets behind them. The next step is to progress towards Stonehenge which is complex and the obstacles are more difficult because the monument was constructed in multiple phases.

Chapter 8: Study As Well As Excavations Of

Stonehenge

In light of the significance and complexity of Stonehenge and the way it has developed over a lengthy period that is not surprising, it has been the subject of a lot of excavations and research. The goal of these investigations is to help resolve the various speculations and theories which have arisen from the mystery about Stonehenge because from the absence of documentation that were left by its creators and its users.

Excavations have been made since 1620.

The first known excavations was carried out around 1620 in 1620 by the Duke of Buckingham following a visit Stonehenge in 1620 by the King James. A survey conducted by architect Indigo Jones at his request by King James was completed shortly after and Jones found out that the stone was built in the time of the Romans.

In 1666, antique historian John Aubrey surveyed the site and found the 56 pits, which were later renamed Aubrey Holes to honor the discovery. Each pit was three feet long and deep they formed a circular shape which was 284 feet in diameter.

In the course of looking at other stone circles, He concluded Stonehenge was not constructed by the Romans according to what Indigo Jones believed and neither by the Danes according to others, but was built by native people. He decided instead that the Druids were the culprits since they were the sole British clergy mentioned in writings from the time.

William Stukeley was next to investigate the site at the beginning of the Eighteenth Century, and he shared the view of Aubrey that Druids were the ones responsible for the construction. His study was more extensive, allowing him to locate those who were responsible for the Avenue, Cursus and various barrows (burial mounds made of stones and earth).

The year 1740 was when Bath designer John Wood created the most complete and accurate plan that has been produced to date. The plan contained the south-west trilithon that fell in 1797, and was then re-elected in the year 1958.

William Cunnington excavated 24 barrows in the early Nineteenth Century, discovering ancient artefacts , and also identifying the location of the Slaughter Stone was located. The remaining 379 barrows of Salisbury Plain were excavated by Richard Colt Hoare.

Flinders Petrie was the first to survey Stonehenge in 1874, and again in 1877. He then established an identification system for Stonehenge that remains in use in the present. In the year 1877 Charles Darwin, as part of his studies into the long-term effects earthworms have on objects in the soil, found that the stones had fallen, and then fell further into the earth because of their activity. His findings were presented in the book The Formation of Vegetable Mould by the Action of Worms.

Twentieth Century and The Start of Restorations

The first major restoration at Stonehenge began in the year 1901 following the fall of some of the stone and its lintel was shattered. The result was concerns about the safety of the other stones, which led to the massive leaning sarsen that was straightened and poured concrete. As part of the project that was led under the supervision of Professor William Gowland, it was that the monument was constructed during the latter part of the Neolithic or the early Bronze Age period.

Additional excavation and restoration work was carried out from 1919-1926, supervised under the command of Lieutenant Colonel William Hawley, when much of the south east portion of Stonehenge was cleared. During this period Hawley excavated the foundations of six stones, as well as the ditch that was in the outer part and also helped relocate those Aubrey Holes. Hawley was reported to have found the entire process quite frustrating, stating that the mystery was getting more complicated the more excavation was carried out.

In 1923, excavations revealed the remains of a man who had been decapitated. The other remains found were cremated bodies from the Neolithic period, whereas this one was an Seventh Century Anglo-Saxon. While the beheading suggests that he was executed The fact that his burial was at Stonehenge might indicate that it was a powerful man or even the throne.

A new series of excavations was carried out from 1950-1964 under the direction of Professor Richard Atkinson, Stuart Piggott and JF Stone. The aim was to answer several unanswered questions, and to stabilize some of the structures and rebuild other features. The knives and axes were found and this enabled the three distinct stages of Stonehenge's construction to be discovered.

In this time, there was the reconstruction of a fallen stone sarsen in the year 1958 that was set on an earthen base to guarantee the stability of the stone in the future. Five years after, another sarsen rock collapsed and was then put back in place with three additional stones.

As part of the preparations for the construction the new tourist facilities further excavations were conducted in the years 1966 and 1967. They discovered the post hole in which a stone which was a partner was located. Heel Stone had been. Additionally, there were a number of Mesolithic hole for posts one of them, the Stonehenge Archer was discovered in the year 1978. The remains were found to be dated at 2300 BC and the archer was an ancestor to the archer 'Amesbury' located about three miles from.

The Stonehenge Environs project, which was conducted in the early 1980s looked at surroundings and were able establish the dates of several features which included The Lesser Cursus and the Coneybury Henge. The Public Accounts Committee conclusion in 1993 that Stonehenge's appearance before the general public as a 'national scandal and a national disgrace was the catalyst for English Heritage to bring together all work that has been done on the site up to. The result was the publication, in the year 1995 of Stonehenge in its natural setting providing the details of every item found on the site.

New Millennium Findings

The excavations, which were led by Prof. Mike Parker Pearson and known collectively as the Stonehenge Riverside Project took place between 2003 and 2008. The primary focus was on nearby monuments as well as their connections to Stonehenge. This included excavations at Durrington Walls and Stonehenge and the discovery of additional stones.

It also in 2008 extracted cremated remains of several areas of Aubrey Holes which was analyzed to reveal they were dug up between 3000 to 2500 BC. In the in the year before, Tim Darvill of the University of Bournemouth and Geoffrey Wainwright of the Society of Antiquaries began excavations within the stone circle. They were able to determine the age of certain bluestones to the time of their construction in 2300 BC and also to discover organic materials dating back to 7700 BC.

The investigation that was conducted is part of SPACES (Strumble-Preseli Early Communities, Environmental Studies and Study) project which examined the bluestone setting to discover the exact source from the bluestones. In addition to an analysis of the geology of bluestones, there was some fieldwork carried out in The Preseli Hills.

Excavating during this time also revealed evidence of Roman activity on the site. The excavations that have taken place over the past several years have revealed a variety of Roman coins, metal objects and pottery pieces.

A second landscape survey in 2009 revealed a small mound believed to be part of the initial monument. The Stonehenge Hidden Landscape Project found in 2010 an henge-like structure just a mile away from the main site . Then next year, they discovered two large pits along the Stonehenge Cursus path. The pits were aligned to the midsummer sun and sunset, when viewed by The Heel Stone.

The southwestern portion of the sarsen circle has no stones, historians and archaeologists have long pondered whether the circle was left unfinished or if some stones were removed prior to the circle's conclusion. The question was answered not by excavation however, but through an in-season drought in 2014 which revealed marks on the grass, which revealed the exact location where stones were previously placed.

In 2014., evidence of nearby wooden and stone structures as well as burial mounds that date to the 4000th year of BC were discovered at researchers at the University of Birmingham. The discoveries are still being made in order that the mysteries about Stonehenge is slowly, but steadily being discovered.

Unanswered Questions Still Unanswered Questions

A lot of questions remain to be addressed through future diggings, research and excavations. This includes the reason Stonehenge was constructed on this particular spot and the exact stone's source. There are numerous questions regarding the method and order of construction as well as whether the stone circle of Sarsen was ever built.

The research has been complicated by the periglacial shift and burrowing of animals which have disturbed the site over a long period of time. This is compounded by poor quality records which usually stem from earlier excavations, and the lack of precise dates that can be verified scientifically.

Yet, there are some new techniques currently being used which were not available to researchers before. This includes digital imagery, mapping in 3D, and carbon dating, which should give greater information than what has been discovered to date. The tale of Stonehenge continues, thus.

The question of whether all the mysteries around Stonehenge are ever resolved remains to be seen as a mystery as they stretch way too far back and have limited evidence. It could be not surprising that some questions are unanswered because having a way to explain everything would deprive the stone of its mystery and the ability to captivate.

The Museum Collections and Records

Excavating to date has revealed a variety of artifacts found at Stonehenge and its surroundings. The majority of these are kept or displayed in The Salisbury Museum or the Wiltshire Museum in Devizes. These museums house almost all the important collections of through the Twentieth Century excavations, although certain of the older ones are still under post-excavation analyses.

The two museums are both recognized to the Museums, Libraries and Archives Council as being the top collections of international and national significance. In addition to their collections, they possess vast archives, documents and an archive of antiquarian materials and documents that provide the background and details of Stonehenge.

Certain items, including William Stukeley's and John Aubrey's manuscripts and papers are accessible at the Bodleian Library in Oxford or the Cambridge's Corpus Christi College.

Many of the items taken from both collections of the Salisbury Museum and the Wiltshire Museum are loaned at the Stonehenge visitor center and are on display there. The visitor center also offers an ongoing program of exhibitions and activities that illustrate the past and unique features of Stonehenge. They include the most recent technologies in audio-visual including digital maps, reconstructions, and demonstrations of the ancient techniques to help make Stonehenge seem alive and relevant even in the present.

Chapter 9: Stonehenge's Position Within

The Landscape

When Stonehenge was in construction Stonehenge was surrounded by chalky grasslands that were utilized by the locals to feed their livestock. There were a few trees, however most of the land was fairly wide.

Stonehenge is situated today within an extensive archaeological context which is mostly attributed to the early Neolithic and late Neolithic and the early Bronze Age developments. The area around Stonehenge is home to several prehistoric sites and more than 350 burial mounds that provide crucial information on how people lived their lives, how society was organized, and also the funerary and ceremonial processions during the period.

Other developments that are near Stonehenge

Alongside Stonehenge in its entirety and the surrounding area, it also contains Stonehenge Cursus, Stonehenge Cursus, Durrington Walls, Woodhenge, Avebury and

Silbury Hill plus numerous other smaller projects. It is a UNESCO World Heritage Site extends across a substantial portion of the area, including numerous sites, in addition to Stonehenge itself. The sites indicate that the entire region was important before Stonehenge was built , and that the creation of so many other monuments in the same area suggests the emergence of a time of intense political and religious rivalry.

The Stonehenge Cursus is also known by The Greater Cursus is a massive ditch and bank earthworks construction which spans 1.9 miles (3 kilometers) and whose width ranges between 330 and 490 feet (100-150 metres). It was constructed between the years 3630 and 3375 B which makes it older than the principal Stonehenge monument.

Cursus Cursus could be an important site for rituals, and was set to coincide with the dawn of spring and the autumn equinoxes. Two pits located near the west and east sides are also aligned with the midsummer sunset and sunrise while barrows have formed inside the Cursus.

Wooden Counterpart

Two miles from the north from Stonehenge are the stone's wood equivalent -- Woodhenge. It was likely built in the 2300s BC and was used up to the year 1800 BC. The site was believed to be a burial mound that was with a bank and ditch measuring 360 feet (110 meters) in diameter , with one entrance towards the north-east. But, these features were completely removed through plowing.

Aerial photos revealed dark spots in a field of wheat and they were later discovered to be sockets empty which held upright timbers. The post holes were laid out in six concentric oval ring which are now marked by concrete posts. The largest of the rings measures by 141 feet (43 by 40 meters) The longer axis of each ring faces towards the summer and winter solstice.

The function of Woodhenge is unclear, however, it is believed to have was used as a place of worship and that the ditches and banks were intended for defense. The timbers could be the foundations of a huge covered structure that had a courtyard in the centre.

At the heart of the grave there were an ossuary of a three-year-old child were discovered. The skull was split open by an axe, which led researchers to believe that the child was sacrificed.

It is believed that a similar structure to Woodhenge might have existed located at Stonehenge prior to its replacement by the massive trilithons and stone circles. The same structures were observed in Durrington Walls, which is just 300 feet (70 metres) away. These structures made of wood could be a marker in the way to the more permanent ones found at Stonehenge or could have served to distinguish the purposes of the various sites -- wood symbolizing life, while stone indicating the passage from life to death.

This is supported by the discovery of bones from pigs found at Woodhenge however none were found at Stonehenge. These bones could indicate that the former was a place that was a place where feasts were held, while Stonehenge was not a site for people living.

Durrington Walls

Durrington Walls was originally developed as a massive wooden circle that measured 500m in diameter and was later reconstructed as a henge during the late Neolithic or the early Bronze Age period. It is believed to have been a companion memorial in the same way as Stonehenge and is believed to be to be the biggest antiquated monument of its kind in Britain.

The henge is one of the largest in the world and was constructed in the 2500 BC in one construction phase. The ditch measured more than 10 metres wide and 5 metres deep, with the dirt extracted from it being utilized to build an external three-metre bank.

The circular timber was aligned to sunrise at midwinter solstice, and therefore was in the opposite alignment as Stonehenge. It is believed that the construction of the circle was never completed, and the posts of the timber were removed to be used in other places.

Evidence of Neolithic houses have been found on Durrington Walls and it is believed that a settlement that could have included up to 1,000 homes that could have accommodated 4,000 people be located there. This could for a while be the largest town in north Europe and could be the place where workers lived that created Stonehenge.

Avebury Henge and Silbury Hill

In the same period that Durrington Walls began to be built and being constructed, the nearby Avebury henge was being built over the span of more than a hundred years. It was comprised of a massive henge with an area of 28.5 metres . It contained inside it a large outer stone circle, as well as two smaller stones at the center in the enclosure.

It is also the biggest megalithic stone circle on earth and initially contained around 100 stones. However, a few of them were destroyed by locals during early Medieval as well as the early Modern times due to religious and practical reasons. They thought they were pagan symbols , or they used the stones for building purposes.

Near Avebury Near Avebury is Silbury Hill, an artificial chalk mound, which was built in phases in the period between 2400-2300 BC. With a height of forty metres and covering an area of around five acres, it's what is the same size as one or two smaller Egyptian pyramids in Giza as well as the highest artificial mound that has been constructed in Europe.

Although the motive behind the hill's construction isn't known the hill would have required immense organisational and technical skills as well as a lot of work to construct. The hill has 324,000 cubic metres (248,000 cubic meters) of materials and it is believed to have required 18 million hours of labour to construct which is equivalent to 500 hundred workers working for 15 years.

Other Events at a Time of Transition

Other notable sites in the area comprise Robin Hood's Ball, a massive sacred and ceremonial causewayed enclosure. It also includes Larkhill an additional causewayed enclosure, which is currently covered by modern military structures. Causewayed enclosures were named due to their ditches crossing causeways.

Larkhill was constructed about 1,150 years prior to the time when the stones were laid out at Stonehenge and was comprised of two circular ditches which were built in sections and extended up to 950 meters in length. Skull bones found in the ditches show that the location was used as a mortuary , while remnants of broken bowls and cow bones indicate that feasting was taking at the site. The discovery of the site in 2016 suggests that there are more prehistoric sites in the area which are yet to be discovered.

These developments took place during a period of massive changes in religion and led to major changes to many of the religious sites. This was also the time of the beginning of what historians refer to as the "Beaker culture" as new cultures, peoples, and customs arrived in Britain.

The influence from the Beaker People

Beaker culture, also known as the Beaker culture, which is more formal called The Bell Beaker culture, was named for the form of the pottery frequently found in their round barrow graves. Beaker people are believed to have originated in Portugal. Beaker culture is thought to have been born in the copper-using region close to the Tagus estuary in Portugal around 2800-2700 BC.

The Beakers have spread across Europe frequently through trade routes to deliver products like axes. In every place they settled they worked as archers, farmers, and metalsmiths, working in gold and copper prior to changing to bronze at the beginning at the beginning of the Bronze Age period. They typically influenced in the areas they resided not only with regards to trade and goods, but also in the realm of beliefs, culture, and religion.

When they first arrived in Britain They were the first metalsmiths and produced their own pottery, weaved garments, and also introduced alcohol-based drinks.

Additionally, to Stonehenge They were also the first to be the first to cremate their dead and to conduct burials for their own in barrows, which were common throughout stonehenge. Stonehenge landscape. Each grave in the barrow was filled with burial objects including daggers, jewelry and pottery to carry the deceased to the afterlife.

An evidence for these practices of burial have been found in abundance in Stonehenge and in the area around. Stone circles that were constructed in the latter part of the Neolithic and the early Bronze Age period are also attributable to the Beaker people, which could be their greatest contribution to Britain.

Beaker culture was also undergoing a transformation. Beaker civilization was a part of the transition from the later Neolithic into the Bronze Age period. The same period, Stonehenge was being transformed to accommodate the huge Sarsen stones and lintels we are seeing today.

The Amesbury Archer -- The King of Stonehenge?

A particularly fascinating find during the early spring of 2002 when making preparations for the building of schools was the discovery of the burial site of an individual who was later to be known as the "Amesbury Archer'. The grave was not just its remains, but those of the man's body but as well gold artefacts and objects that made it the most affluent Bronze Age burial site yet discovered to date.

The grave lies about two miles to the south of Stonehenge and is not too far distant from Durrington Walls. The analysis of the remains suggests that the man was from central Europe however some of the jewelry and pottery found at the burial site are believed to be from European source.

The objects found in the grave include a guard for the wrist which indicated the archer's high rank, a knife made of copper, Beaker pots, arrow heads, and gold jewelry. The value and quality of the items found in the grave, which totals nearly one hundred pieces are much greater than the ones from similar sites. They show that the man immense wealth and ability.

The radiocarbon dates of the remains suggests that the man was alive in the period between 2400-2200 BC at the time the enormous stone circles and the avenue leading to the River Avon were being built. This, in conjunction with the Archer's ancestry and apparent wealth, has resulted in some calling him the "King of Stonehenge as they believe the archer was part of a ruling class. However, there is not any evidence to back this notion.

Military Connections

The modern structures that were beginning to take over the site during the 1920s have been taken away. In the past, as recently as 100 years ago, it was reported that an airfield from the First World War airfield was constructed in the area that lies between the visitor center and the ancient stonework.

Pilots were taught there prior to they were transferred to Western Front. Thus, fighter planes circulated over the monument, and there were crashes close to the monument.

It is believed that the Salisbury Plain area has long been linked to the military, with documents that show Royal Engineers reconnaissance balloons taking part in training exercises since the 1880s. Then there was The War Office acquiring areas of land surrounding the Stonehenge monument. Thankfully, all indications that refer to an airfield has since been taken down and Stonehenge is now in peace.

Chapter 10: Stonehenge Folklore

The long-running history of Stonehenge and the general aura of mystery surrounding the site, it's not surprising that a variety of myths have been related to Stonehenge.

One of the stories stems from the conviction that Stonehenge was constructed as a monument to the fallen nobles. The idea was suggested in the writings of Geoffrey of Monmouth in the Twelfth century as a part of his publication History of the Kings of Britain and provides an unorthodox explanation of the method by which Stonehenge was constructed.

He believed that Stonehenge's stones were healing stones which had been taken into Ireland in Africa through giants. Stonehenge was selected during the Fifth Century as the site to honor the 3,000 nobles who had been killed by Saxons during the battle. The king Aurelius Ambrosius led Merlin along with his brother, the King's father Uther Pendragon along with 1500 knights Ireland to recover the stones.

The Magic of Merlin Moves the Stones

They killed 7700 Irish in the fight, but they were unable to transfer the stone. Merlin however succeeded through magic and carried the stones aboard ships to England to be erected at Stonehenge. King Aurelius Ambrosius as well as others were burial there. If the story is true, it would result in Stonehenge being constructed around 2,000 years later than the widely accepted date.

Another legend tells of the brutal murder of the 420 Brythonic soldiers by the invaders under the leadership of King Hengist. In remorse over the act, Hengist constructed Stonehenge as a memorial.

The Legend of the Heel Stone

Another folk tale is about The Heel Stone, also previously called the "Friar's Heel as well as the "Sun Stone"The latter is likely refers to the idea that the sunrise on the solstice of summer is visible over the stone when it is viewed from the stone's circular. The story recounts the story of how the Devil purchased the stones from the woman from Ireland and then brought they into Salisbury Plain.

The stones were believed to be obtained through trickery, with the Devil promises to give the woman the amount of gold she could possibly count within how long it would take him transport them. Since they were transported immediately to England using magical powers and the woman was left with no time to calculate any gold, and the Devil took the stones in exchange for nothing.

One stone did fall in the River Avon, the rest were safe and the Devil claimed that no one could ever find their source or according to the story of the story, not be able to determine how many stones. A friar who heard the story to doubt this incident, the Devil dropped a stone which was thrown at the friar's heel and then was sunk into the ground, which is where it remains to this day.

The story is believed to be the work of Geoffrey of Monmouth however his description of the creation of Stonehenge has little in common with. While the tale is obviously, a work of fiction The Heel Stone does bear what is believed to be the footprint of the footprint of a foot.

Giants and Aliens

One theory concerning Stonehenge could be that the site was constructed by giants, known as the Nephilin who were nearly completely destroyed by the flood that was associated in Noah and his Ark. They relied on their immense size and strength to move and raise the stones. This , to a certain degree, align to the Merlin theory, as there is a photo dating back to early in Fourteenth Century that shows a huge stone helping Merlin to construct Stonehenge.

However, there is no evidence of physical proof to support this, and it is dismissed as a myth. Another myth that is easily dismissed is the myth that says the stones of Stonehenge are actually made up of giants who were transformed into stone by dancing in the circle.

The most intriguing theories of the way Stonehenge was constructed is that god-like aliens gave the necessary information to the human race. The same knowledge was utilized to construct other massive old structures, like those of the Moai head located on Easter Island and the pyramids in Egypt.

While all of these stories are not believable as true, they often represent the prevalent beliefs of the time, and could contain a small base of truth to them. But none, in the end will diminish the mystery that persists around Stonehenge.

Stonehenge Today

Stonehenge is nowadays a popular tourist attraction which attracts tourists from all over the globe. It is classified as a World Heritage Site, is part of the Crown and is managed through English Heritage, with the surrounding land owned by The National Trust, and has been legally protected as a Scheduled Ancient Monument since 1882. Therefore, it appears it is in good hands however that doesn't mean it is immune to debate and controversy It is far from it.

The access to the stones has been limited since 1977, and visitors are restricted to them only during the solstices of winter and summer or by booking special tickets. Traffic is also kept out as visitors take their 1.5 mile (2.1 kilometers) journey to the visitor center by foot or via shuttle bus. The system is complemented by the use of a timed ticketing system which is supposed to prevent excessive numbers of visitors in the centre at any given time , and will ensure an enjoyable visit.

They replaced the previous train fleet - which were carriages that were pulled with Land Rovers. The shuttle buses were pulled out of service due to difficulties in turning around the monument and the visitor centre, which was allegedly due to the doors of the carriages being located on the wrong side, preventing an easy alignment with the platforms.

The New Visitor Centre and The Dangers of Over-Commercialisation

The visitor center is fairly brand new, and was completed in 2013 with a cost around PS27 million. The facility replaced facilities that were not adequate and included a dismal building, portable toilets , and an uninviting tunnel that ran under the road that led to the Stonehenge site. The new site is a cutting-edge facility that houses the traditional ticketing area, cafe, and the obligatory gift shop, in addition to exhibits and displays designed to inform and familiarize visitors with the Stonehenge's history and background.

Since Stonehenge has attracted more than 1.3 million tourists in the year 2016, which is a 1.1 percent increase over the previous year, the overall method can be seen as an incredible achievement. Nevertheless, it has its share of critics, many of whom focus on the over-commercialisation of the site.

If this is the case then it could be exemplified through the replica Neolithic dwellings that have been built in the vicinity of the visitor centre. They are designed to show how people lived amidst the ruins of 4,500 years ago, and were constructed using authentic methods and materials. They also show traditional household skills, such as grinding grains and making ropeshowever, the whole concept is too much for those who want an authentic experience.

It's the Problem of the Roads

One of the biggest issues that is associated with Stonehenge has been the closeness of two frequented roads: The A344 that runs between Andover and Warminster to the north , and the A303 Basingstoke to Honiton road that runs south. These roads were a one of the reasons identified in the National Geographic Condition Survey published in 2006, which placed Stonehenge 75th out of the top 94 World Heritage Sites and said it was in moderate danger'.

Both roads pass close to Stonehenge and since Stonehenge was declared an World Heritage Site, there were plans to upgrade the A303 and also to close the A344 to ensure that the views from the stones are enhanced. Rerouting roads is costly and a variety of plans were proposed and abandoned in the past. However, the approval for the visitor centre that was built which was approved by the state in 2009, coincided with the closing of A344.

The centre's planning permission has been granted from Wiltshire Council the following year and the center was constructed with the help by an PS10 million Heritage Lottery Fund grant. The day before the visitor center opened in 2013, the A344 was shut down on the 23rd June 2013, and work began to clear it and re-grass the area.

The most recent plan to ease traffic congestion is focusing upon the A303. It is the main trunk road connecting London up to West Country and runs within about 165 meters of the landmark. It's a single-carrier road at this point, resulting in congestion, with the inherent issue of noise and pollution, which makes it difficult for pedestrians to access the landscape around.

The Controversy surrounding the Proposed Tunnel

The 12th of June, 2017 the Transport Minister Chris Grayling announced plans to transform the A303 to a dual carriageway and with an approximate cost in the region of PS1.4 billion, the plan is to run it through tunnels underneath the road. This 1.7-mile-long tunnel will be part of a larger road-improvement plan which aims to provide a better connection to M3, the A303, M3 and M5 in addition to improving circulation and helping the local economy at an estimated price in the region of PS2 billion.

The tunnel is a long-standing concept, first proposed in 1989. The most recent version has been welcomed from Historic England as an investment in the nation's heritage. In addition, the UNESCO World Heritage organisation has accepted the plan in principle and the idea is backed from English Heritage and the National Trust and the National Trust, both of whom think it will improve knowledge and appreciation of the landmark. There are a lot of people who are against the planned development.

There is a concern that, since the road that will replace it will actually be more wide and include slip-roads, that the road's surface is likely to be larger. A different option is to convert the current A303 one-way road westbound and then construct an eastbound route at a distance from Stonehenge. This would be cheaper and reduce by half the amount of traffic, however it's unlikely to gain approval.

The historians and archaeologists are of the opinion that the tunnel may cause harm to the monument and general landscape. Others believe it's wrong to attempt to reverse the course of history. They claim it is not a good idea to do so. A303 is currently one of the roads in the Stonehenge area and must not be overlooked by putting grass over the current road, and obscuring that new route. It's like trying to go back to earlier times and trying to create an environment that is believed to be authentic for Stonehenge that is a nigh-on impossible idea.

There's even a belief that tunneling could keep the stones hidden from the public, The only method that they can see the stones is to pay an entry cost to the Stonehenge site. It is evident that any decision made will not be a hit with everyone and could be the continuation of Stonehenge's intriguing and sometimes controversial history.

Chapter 11: Short Overview Of The Major

Phases Of Stonehenge

Stonehenge was a landmark on the soaring Salisbury Plain for thousands of years. Recent excavations of the site have revealed the constantly changing facade of this amazing landmark. Through massive changes, this ionic stone temple was built over several periods.

Phase I The bluestone circles, between c3100 and 2935 BC

The ditch was circular and the bank (henge) approximately 6 feet in height was built. Within the bank, 56 circular pits - known as the Aubrey Holes were dug. They contained bluestones and cremations. A stone circle dubbed Bluehenge, which was made up of 30 stones about 6ft high was located about 1 mile away from the River Avon at the end of the Avenue. Another bluestone circle is situated in Fargo Wood. The source of bluestone is believed to be from the Preseli Mountains in Wales. But, according Professor Rob Ixer's tantalizing new evidence by stone chippings discovered near the western edge of the Cursus suggests that the bluestones could be derived from further away, perhaps from Snowdonia or as well as the Llyn Peninsula and Anglesey. Archaeologist Michael Parker Pearson

Additional bluestone circles

A number of bluestone circles were erected within the vicinity of Stonehenge. Bluehenge was situated close to Stonehenge's River Avon one mile away to the south-east of Stonehenge.

West of Stonehenge near Fargo Wood stood yet another stone circle. A further bluestone circle could have been erected in Coneybury Henge from 3254 - 2911 BC.

1 has discovered another stone hole near Stonehenge near Coneybury Henge which may have contained another circle of bluestone. Interestingly, when polished, the dark bluestones, with their distinct silver flecks could look like the star-spangled heavens. We'll soon discover this Heel Stone was initially used as a lunar marker stone,

which was used to map the moon's complex cycle.

Phase II Phase II: ca. 2500 BC

The entrance was widening to roughly align it with Heel Stone with the summer solstice dawn and an earthen road, which connected into the River Avon around a mile away, was built. Two bluestone rings were built in the middle of Stonehenge. The world famous sarsen-lintelled stone circle with thirty stones and five enormous trilithons made the most iconic stone circle in Britain. The four station stones that made up the shape of a rectangle were placed on the outside within the circle.

Phase III Phase III: c2400 BC

The bluestones were then returned and placed in a ring inside the sarsen circular and 19 formed a horseshoe-shaped shape inside the trilithons. In the middle, is the Altar Stone was erected and the Slaughter Stone and its counterpart were placed along the causeway. In the 1600s BC two pits in two rings

The 'Y' and holes for the 'Z' were dug in the sarsen circle, but the work was not completed.

The Moon in midwinter

A variety of astronomical alignments was expertly included into the megalithic structures which established a close connection with and the Sun, Moon and the standing stones. For example, in Phase I the Heel Stone was first elevated for marking the Mid-Swing location in the moon's Metonic cycle around Midwinter.

In the Moon's intricate Metonic period of 18.61 years at the exact midpoint that the full moon will be visible above the horizon, and then appear over the crest that taper of the Heel Stone. From the mid-swing point, the moonrises gradually shift towards the right until it reaches the 'standstill' point, which takes 56 months before returning towards the Heel Stone in the same time frame. Similar cycles occur when the moon rises and transitions to the left of the Heel Stone and gives an 18.61 year Metonic cycle.

In the 1920s, Colonel Hawley discovered six postholes that ran across the causeway. These were read by amateur astronomer C.A. Peter Newham as temporary devices for spotting by Neolithic men to map and track the Moon's complex cycle. The causeway's entry point

Also, it was modified

in order to make sure that the banks

aligned with

Moon's main and

minor standstill

positions and thus

Framed the entire

Metonic cycle

Right.

It is the Heel Stone and the Moon's intricate cycle.

The Sun in midsummer

About 2500 BC the ancient lunar entrance was altered. The causeway's entrance was expanded approximately in alignment with to align the Heel Stone to the midsummer sunrise. The focus had changed towards that of the Moon towards the Sun.

The archaeological evidence discovered through Mike Pitts suggests that the Heel Stone once had a solar counterpart. If this is the case the solstice would have been a stunning sequence could have taken place. On the morning of the Summer Solstice the sun would be rising on the central axis the Avenue. A spectacular corridor of sunlight caused from the Heel Stone and its partner could penetrate the sacredness of the stone circle , striking it with the Altar Stone and so declaring the solstice ceremonies.

Along the same axis, the setting midwinter sun slowly fades into the horizon, in the opposite direction of sunrise on the Summer Solstice sunrise. The five massive trilithons that were constructed in a horseshoe-shaped shape, increase in height toward the south-west and towards the midwinter sunset. The sun's setting is beautifully captured by the tallest trilithon.

It is an intricate design canon, which was built around 4500 years ago.

Second phase Stonehenge has been dedicating to the Sun that was once regarded all over the world as the source of life, the source of all power and prosperity.

The ancient sites that surround Stonehenge

Nearby Stonehenge There are a myriad of ancient sites, like Neolithic causewayed enclosures, that were built prior to the stone circle. There are also contemporary Bronze Age burial mounds, many of which contain remarkable discoveries as well as Iron Age forts which crown the hills surrounding them.

Normanton Up 2500 - 1500 BC

(OS MAP 184.115413)

A trackway is located at the

west of Stonehenge

It crosses the A303.

that, after a brief

Walk around

Two-thirds of

mile will lead to

finest Bronze

Age cemetery in

Britain. "A great

Barrows in a group

that are running in the direction of

south-east until north

west, with a variety of

Their shape their form, perfect

in their in their

and wealthy and wealthy

contents', declared

Sir, the antiquarian

Richard Colt Hoare

in 1808. The barrows were discovered in 1808. Colt Hoare found faience beads from Egypt, Kimmeridge shale from Dorset and amber found along in the North Sea coast revealing that different trades took place.

The Bush barrow is a gold mine that has been incredibly spectacular.

When you reach the floor

from of Bush Barrow,

On Normanton Down,

Colt Hoare found

the most affluent grave

products from prehistoric times

Britain. He

discovered an skull

of a tall and stout

man who is lying on the ground

South towards North with

A gold lozenge

A breast-shaped breast plate

and a dagger that is inlaid

with metal (shown

below) and below) and

bronze axe, mace

and shield. Other

gold objects were

discovered in barrows

close by, for example, nearby, such as red

amber set with intricate detail

with gold, and then polished

The bone is also incorporated

with gold. at the time of

Golden Barrow,

Upton Lovell, near

Warminster, Colt

Hoare discovered a golden cone with 1000 amber beads, which are worth more than gold. The above illustration is adapted from the original drawings of Colt Hoare.

The Greater Cursus (OS MAP 184.124430)

The Greater Cursus is believed to date back to 3800 BC that was a huge enclosure that was about half of a mile (800m) north of Stonehenge. It was comprised of two banks that were roughly parallel and ditches spanning 310 feet (100m) from the course of the monument spanned about two mile (3km). They get their name from the antiquarian of the 18th century, William Stukeley, who believed they were Roman races. The word "cursus" is Latin for movement and running. Nowadays, there is little evidence of the once massive monument that was roughly aligned East - West to face the sunrise of the equinox. Another alignment that was noted by the archaeologist Aubrey Burl, points out that the Cursus is located on one of the bank areas along with Avon River. River Avon.

The western part is sketched in the work of William Stukeley and is shown above. On the eastern side, there is a large barrow that is seriously damaged.

In the beginning, the Cursus would have been white and its chalk banks would have sparkled in the moon and sun light. There are other cursuses throughout Britain one of the biggest that is located in Dorset and runs over seven miles (10km). Half an inch (800m) to the north and west of Stonehenge Cursus was once the Lesser Cursus, now ploughed out. It ran for about a quarter mile (400m).

The Cursus barrows. The first time they were opened was by Lord Pembroke in 1722.

The Heel Stone

The Heel Stone marked the movements of both the Sun as well as the Moon. Every year, the midwinter Moon appears above the tapering crest of Heel Stone often coinciding with an eclipse. Also, each midsummer, the Sun would roughly align in a similar way to Heel Stone. According to certain archaeologists they believe that the Sun was able to rise in the vicinity of Heel Stone and its partner, Stone 97 (now missing) creating a magnificent dark corridor that would enter the inner circle before striking on the center Altar Stone, announcing the longest day of the year, and surely it would signal the beginning of rituals.

The Woodhenge (OS MAPS 184.150434)

This location was thought to be a barrow that was flattened until the Squadron Chief Insall made a series aerial photos that revealed white circular marks (now depicted

through the concrete post). Woodhenge

was an essential component of the

Stonehenge landscape.

Built around

4200 years ago This was

Early Bronze Age

The site was comprised

of six ovals

concentric timber

posts are surrounded

by a ditch , and

the outer bank, and it was

damaged by the entrance

causeway to the north-east of the country causeway to the north-east

in the general direction of midsummer sunrise. The massive timber posts could be wooden versions that were similar to Stonehenge located one miles away (1.5km). It is believed that Ring C was the very first of a series of posts that were constructed - 16 posts of one-metre thickness each of them weighing 5 tons were placed in an oval-shaped design.

In the wooden ring stood the burial site of a 3-year-old boy who might have died of trauma into the head. Numerous scholars have thought that the child may have been an act of sacrifice.

New Discovery

One mile to the south to the south of Amesbury archaeologists have found the remains of a wood circle that resembles Woodhenge with concentric circles similar to those.

The grave of flint that covers the tiny child.

There is the Cuckoo Stone and Durrington Walls

(OS MAP 184.150437)

In the western part of Woodhenge is an erect Cuckoo Stone, which was once in a straight line, possibly to mark a waypoint towards Stonehenge. In close proximity is Durrington Walls which lies approximately one mile to the north-east of Stonehenge. In the early Neolithic (c2600 BC) a huge circular village, perhaps the largest in Europe was located in the area that is shown below.

The archaeological evidence suggest that the town could have been used by people who constructed Stonehenge. Numerous houses, some with hearths or beds made of wooden furniture and storage and larders, have been discovered. It is believed that 300 houses could remain under the henge bank , and are waiting for the next excavations.

About around 2500 BC the

The area was transformed

and the biggest and the largest

all over the world

constructed. It comprised

of a depth of 16ft (5.5m) deep

A ditch as well as an external

bank, and in the

There were two rings on the site

huge timber posts.

The super

henge had four entrances

of which, the north and the north

the south was the only ones to be blocked.

in the 2000s BC.

Archaeologists are of the opinion that

The south entrance was the main one.

from Woodhenge. Today

very little is known about this

former super-henge. The Henge Monument.

Figsbury Rings (OS MAP 184.188338)

The hill fort, which is circular and covers six hectares of land is in guardianship of the National Trust. Archaeologists have noticed that the style that the fort has is completely distinct from the other forts on hills. The image above shows that the bank's outer along with the ditch, are divided by a large flat area , which is separated from an inner ditch that has an embankment. The inner ditch ranges in width , ranging from around 42 feet (13m) and 19ft (6m) as well as the ditch measures 48 feet (15m) to 10 feet (3.6m) wide and deep. Because of the unique style of the complex, some question whether it was an actual hill fort, but rather an event site, like causewayed enclosures or Henge monuments.

The earthworks are extremely defensive and protect Maiden Castle in Dorset.

Yarnbury Castle, Steeple Langford

(OS MAP 184.035404)

Near Stonehenge close to Stonehenge is Yarnbury Castle, one of the most beautiful hill forts in Wiltshire and one of the most well-preserved of the hill forts on the plateau. The fort was visited by the famous Sir Richard Colt Hoare in the 19th century, the fort's history has not changed much. Below is an illustration from the book of Colt Hoare The Ancient History of Wiltshire Vol I. The circular earthworks stand out and cover approximately 10.5 acres. The fort is protected by two defense banks that are about 22 feet (7.5m) high, with deep ditches. The earthworks were constructed for slinging stone warfare. There are evidence of a third earthwork, which was designed as an outer defence with an in-turned entrance to the east. It was about 28ft (9m) across, and featuring elaborate earthworks spotted in the work of Colt Hoare and clearly marked in the drawing. Inside the fort , there are remnants of an older enclosure that measured approximately 3.5 acres with an entry in the western part.

From the 18th century to 1916, an annual fair for sheep was held on the 4th of October within the fort on the hill. The sheep pens can be seen along the eastern edge of the enclosed area.

Ogbury Camp, Durnford (OS MAP 184.143383)

In the Iron Age many different types of hill forts were built. We have seen impressive defensive structures like Maiden Castle and Yarnbury Castle and possibly a ceremonial center situated at Figsbury Rings. Ogbury Camp is yet another illustration of how varied hill forts could be. It covers 25 acres and has little to offer in terms of defense, that has led scientists to believe that it could be constructed to serve as a corral for animals, or as a ceremonial Druid center.

The Vespasian Camp

Although it's located situated on private property Vespasian's Camp is closest hill fort located to Stonehenge. An enormous fort that is almost oval in shape with two massive banks. On the east side there is Gay's Cave, a grotto or cave-like feature. It is believed that this that it is the place the place where John Gay wrote The Beggar's Opera.

Winkelbury Camp, Berwick St John

(OS MAP 184.952218)

Below below is Winkelbury Camp, an unfinished hill fort with five hectares of land that was protected by two ditches and banks separated by a huge opening. In the later years, about 250 BC an additional ditch and bank were built around the hill's spur but they were never finished, and today, it's possible to observe the unfinished materials dumped onto the surface.

About 50 BC the size of the fort was drastically reduced when it was isolated from the northern portion by a curving banks and ditch. The entrance is at the eastern part of the bank, and another to the north. The final changes could be a plan to build up the fort in the event that the Roman Legions progressed.

Many hill forts have entrances that have a view of the rising sun and it's tempting believe that during this time of the year, the massive wooden gates for entrance were opened wide to allow sunlight to be able to enter the fort, reiterating the customs of the past. It is interesting to note that other hill forts within the region are also equipped with entrances that seem to be facing toward the midsummer rising Sun for instance, Bratton Castle and Scratchbury Camp and another entrance inside Liddington Castle, near Swindon has a view of the Midwinter sunrise.

Old Sarum, near Salisbury

(OS MAP 184.137327)

Amazing Iron Age hill

Fort, which is dominated

through an Norman motte.

The echoes of the past

is easily accessible

Within the grounds:

The foundations of an ancient

cathedral, castle and

bishop's palace dating

to circa 1068 - 78 AD.

The hill fort is a basic ditch and bank with an entrance to the east. Excavated pits include storage along with pottery and numerous brooches. Old Sarum could be the site of The Roman Station of Sorviodunum however, experts believe that it was located in the west or south. Numerous Roman roads that ran through the south-west were documented in the writings of Colt Hoare and are shown below.

Winterbourne Stoke (OS MAP 184.101416)

The ancient city is situated close by.

Ridgeway, Winterbourne Stoke is

one of the most striking and impressive

preserved cemeteries from prehistoric times in

Britain comprises a Neolithic

Barrows with a long length and many Bronze Age

round barrows with different shapes

and in various sizes. Winterbourne Stoke Round barrows situated to the west are displayed in the above image.

The Neolithic long barrow

The oldest monuments found in the landscape are the long barrows, which were built between 3200 and 4000 BC before the bank and ditch at Stonehenge. The barrows were orientated to face the midsummer sun, the long barrow in Winterbourne Stoke is 250ft (70m) long and 10ft tall (3.6m) with adjacent ditches on both sides. Most long barrows found in Wessex are used to hold communal burials, however, this one is unusual in that it was only a single male skeleton near the northern part. In a later time there were several burials inserted into the mound. one female and a male and four infants in the typical Bronze Age foetal position.

Barrows of unusual round bronze age from 2500 to 1500 BC

Take a stroll around Winterbourne Stoke Bronze Age cemetery and you'll be able to see the most common kinds of round barrows located in Wessex! There are two lines of circular bars are located in the north-east direction from the long barrow, consisting of bell disc, pond and bell barrows, as well as nineteen bowl bars. Additional barrow clusters that are slightly towards from the northern part of the one comprise of five bowl barrows as well as saucer barrows. The first bowl barrows were constructed in the year 2000 BC and were used for female or male burials. The majority of burial mounds found are found in Stonehenge's Stonehenge landscape were discovered during the 18th century and discovered by Richard Colt Hoare. A large number of the items found are on display in the Devizes and Salisbury Museums. The images of the round and long barrows were taken from Colt Hoare's book 'Ancient Wiltonshire 1812.

White Barrow, Tilshead, Salisbury Plain

(OS MAP 184.033468)

One of the most well-preserved lengthy barrows of Wiltshire is located on National Trust land which is accessible all year long and is accessible for free. The mound dates back to 3800 BC and with an east-west orientation, the mound is 255 feet (78m) long and 155 feet (47.6m) in width and is 9ft (2.7m) high at its eastern edge. The ditch to its western edge is 4 feet (1.2m) wide and is perfectly preserved. The site was discovered in the hands of Colt Hoare in the nineteenth century, but there was nothing aside from the black earth layer which could be the remains of a wood mortuary chamber as well as some antler pieces. Burial chambers made of wood were prevalent across Salisbury Plain utilizing the local woods sources.

Megalithic long barrows

17 miles further to the North lies Avebury Henge, a gigantic megalithic complex. Within the region are numerous long barrows that include megalithic chambers. West Kennet long barrow, close to Avebury It is restored and impressive with five megalithic inner chambers. The Sarsen Stone Deposits were abundant throughout the Avebury surroundings, and some of them can be found in Piggledene OS map

173.143686 and Lockeridge dene OS map 173.144674. Sandstone boulders are remnants of the former cap for the chalk during remote times. It is interesting to note that the holes in the rocks were created by the roots of palm trees! The stones from Sarsen were brought to Stonehenge for the purpose of creating the lintelled circular feature and the horseshoe-shaped inner feature.

West Kennet long barrow near Avebury, Wiltshire contains five chambers in stone, which were used to store burial remains. Access is free and accessible throughout the year long. OS MAP 173.104677

Map of Stonehenge's Stonehenge Environs:

Displaying Woodhenge, Durrington Walls, Normanton Down, The Cursus, Ogbury Camp, Vespasian's Camp, Winterbourne Stoke barrows and the important Bronze Age burial cemeteries.

20

Utilize this illustrated guide to discover Stonehenge and the many other ancient sites that are situated around the stone circle.

Explore the sites of the newly excavated areas: Bluestone circles

The alignment of the stars at Stonehenge

Durrington Walls village and finds

Woodhenge along with the Cuckoo stone

The Curse

Figsbury Rings

Old Sarum

Ogbury Camp

Yarnbury Castle and Old Sarum

Roman Roads to the West

Normanton Down and the Bush Barrow discovers

Conclusion

"Pile of Stone-henge!" So proud to hint at but keep

The secrets of your heart, that thou love to be able to hear

The Plain is booming to the whirlwind's sweeping,

The inmate of Nature's endless year."

This passage from the poem written by William Wordsworth in 1793 "Guilt and sadness; or events on Salisbury Plain," indicates, Stonehenge has captured people's imaginations for a long time. In a way, the task appears easy, considering that Stonehenge is an impressive ancient monument as well as a world heritage site as well as a sacred site. Yet, many questions remain regarding the people who built it: their history, their identity and lifestyle and their motivations for building Stonehenge, and the methods they employed. Although archaeology has provided insights into the answers to these questions and probably more than anyone could had predicted just a few years ago, it is safe to say that we'll never be able to know everything we can about Stonehenge. In a way all the mystery layers and doubt enhance the appeal of the place. In the same way the idea that Stonehenge is an "living temple" is a reason for some people are drawn to Stonehenge is not in connection with the latest discoveries made through ground-penetrating radar.

The 20th century's story of the festival has been an era of conflict as well as exclusion and accusation but the tides seem to be changing. The era of the six-week Free Festivals will likely be gone forever Hippies and Druids are back to celebrate the Solstice celebrations. Sometimes the pagans as well as scientists collaborated in tandem. From the beginning of 1986, the archaeologist Christopher Chippindale called for a compromise and a gentle approach to negotiations. nowadays, a lot of neo-pagans are fascinated by the work archaeologists are required to contribute. They keep track of the latest excavation developments, argue about what should be done with the excavated bodies and are even willing to participate in excavations and archaeology experiments.

All indications indicate that things will only get improved in Stonehenge in the coming years. The celebrations of religious significance and the raucous ones have been able to be found in the same space as serious research and a wide-eyed tourist. New archaeological discoveries, like the two henges in the vicinity as well as the neolithic settlement found at Durrington Walls, promise to increase our understanding of neolithic people and what they believed, as well as providing the potential for the future discovery of.

Finally, the area is getting the reverence it deserves. The road leading to the site is slowly disappearing. and the clay grasslands will be rehabilitated and a visitor center that includes a museum and rebuilt village will be constructed. It's been a thrilling century of exploration as well as celebration and conflict throughout the century, and Stonehenge has stood as a an unmoving witness. Apart from the neolithic time period of the builders, there's never been an ideal time to explore or study Stonehenge.

www.ingramcontent.com/pod-product-compliance
Lightning Source LLC
Chambersburg PA
CBHW050027130526
44590CB00042B/2040